Executive Presence
for the Modern Leader

D1637382

Executive Presence

FOR THE

Modern Leader

A Guide to Cultivating
Success and Thriving
in the Workplace

D. A. BENTON

ROCKRIDGE
PRESS

Interior and Cover Designer: Regina Stadnik / Richard Tapp
Art Producer: Tom Hood
Editor: Jed Bickman
Production Editor: Andrew Yackira
Production Manager: Martin Worthington

Author photograph courtesy Mary Harrison

Shutterstock pp. ii, viii, xii, 11, 12, 31, 32, 60, 87, 88, 105, 106, 127, 128, 143, 144

Hardcover ISBN: 978-1-63878-588-0 | Paperback ISBN: 978-1-64876-928-3
eBook ISBN: 978-1-64876-929-0

R1

To Jim Bowman

Contents

Introduction

My parents were small-town grocery store owners, later adding a movie theater and a drugstore to their business portfolio. As they worked together in ventures, I was raised around the business operations, so I got to observe adults outside my family beginning at an early age.

Because I was always at the grocery store, my parents had the idea of giving me my own playhouse right in the middle of the store—a safe and contained space where they could watch over me. It was a promotional house-shaped cardboard box from the Keebler cookie company. From inside my four-by-four-foot hideaway, I could peer out and watch people as they shopped and as they gossiped about each other. It was a small town, and everyone had an opinion about everyone else. *What was it about someone that informed others' opinions of them?* I wondered in fascination. In my little brain, I could tell there were things about some people that caused them to get more positive attention than others, and I decided I wanted some of that for myself.

Everything I did—teenage jobs, college education, outside activities, and personal entrepreneurial ventures—focused around meeting people and observing behaviors that seemed to set some people dramatically apart in the business world.

Two years into my first job out of college, I was the sole woman on a team of men. One Monday morning, my boss called me into his office and said, "I have to let you go. It's not that you're not working hard enough or aren't smart or aren't contributing, but it's because of this . . ." He lifted up his right hand and rubbed his thumb and index and middle fingers together. "It's this fuzzy stuff I can't quite put my finger on, but that's the problem."

But was he right? I was a female island in a sea of men in this company, and I didn't know any code of behavior. I just tried to work hard, get results on time, and stay on budget. But I didn't know how to schmooze or stand out in a positive way. I didn't even know how to fit in. After getting fired from that first job, I decided I needed to learn.

Because I had grown up with entrepreneurs, I decided to start my own venture. I wanted to be around CEOs—the kind who exemplified success in business. I started a little company called All Around Girls (a name that fit the code of appropriateness at the time but might not anymore). My brochure explained that I provided services to CEOs that their secretaries didn't have time to do. For an hourly rate, I would advertise the car they wanted to sell, buy Christmas presents, arrange for an artist to sketch a colleague's home to be given as a gift, plan a party, or go to their private airplane hangar and help the designer redecorate. I completed whatever task needed to be done within the caveat printed on the brochure: "anything legal, moral, and ethical." And with that, I got to go behind the scenes in the lives of big bosses.

In conjunction with my new venture, I took on a personal research project. Every time I got to talk to a CEO, I asked them, "If two people start in their careers with similar experience, intelligence, and ambition, why, over time, does one get to this level and one only get to that?" I'd demonstrate with my hands, lifting one hand a little high and the other hand much higher.

After posing this question to several hundred CEOs, I felt I had broken the code, so I called a *Chicago Tribune* columnist and explained, "I have some research findings your readers might be interested in." He listened to my pitch, liked it, and wrote about it. He labeled this ability "executive charisma." I called it "executive presence." The day the article came out, two CEOs contacted me to help them with their own executive presence. With that, I immediately closed the doors on All Around Girls and started Benton Management Resources to teach others how to access their own executive presence.

I've now spent 40 years continuing my study of executive leadership presence in order to coach executives. I also teach at the university level. I've coached and presented to executives in 18 different countries and in many more cultures than that. This is my 13th book on the subject. In this ever-changing world, I've continued to learn for myself and share with others how to fit in but also stand out in the business world:

to be memorable, impressive, credible, genuine, trusted, confident, and competent.

This book will work for you whether you are an aspiring or current leader, whether you are hoping to land a great job, thrive in your current role, or secure a promotion. It will help you build the career you dream of. This is the most up-to-date, accessible, and practical guide to developing your own executive presence to thrive in the ever-changing workplace. The lessons I've learned have given me a very good life, and I hope they provide the same to you.

CHAPTER ONE

Executive Presence

You're smart, hardworking, and honest. Shouldn't that be enough for career success? Yes, it's important to be those things, but it's not sufficient. You also need to set yourself apart from all the other people who can say the same. Unfortunately, you don't get to make all your own decisions in your career—you can't decide when you deserve a promotion or whether you get hired for a new job; those decisions are anchored in others' perceptions of you.

There is an unwritten code of behavior among successful executives. They don't admit it. It's almost as if they don't want to talk about it for fear of jinxing it. They may even deny that a code of behavior exists. But it's there. It's executive presence. It doesn't matter how you feel about it; what matters is how your colleagues perceive you. The good news is that it can be learned. Syndicated cartoonist Ashleigh Brilliant noted in his book *I May Not Be Perfect, but Parts of Me Are Excellent*, "I wish I had been born with an unfair advantage instead of having to try to acquire one." Clearly, not all of us grew up in country clubs caddying for the people who someday would hire us into great jobs. The rest of us deserve the advantage, too, and we know we're going to have to work for it. So let's learn how.

Leaders with Presence

Profile: Chris Lighty

Manager Chris Lighty was one of the pioneers who made hip-hop into a big business. His clients included LL Cool J, Mariah Carey, A Tribe Called Quest, Busta Rhymes, Missy Elliott, and Sean Combs.

He grew up right along with hip-hop: In the Bronx, he started out carrying crates of records for DJ Red Alert. From there, he became the road manager for Boogie Down Productions and then worked at Def Jam Recordings before leaving to form his own agency, Violator. Lighty died tragically in 2012, but not before he changed hip-hop forever.

Imagine him at a pivotal moment in his career: He's trying to sign a deal with Aftermath Records—Dr. Dre's label—for his client, 50 Cent (Curtis Jackson), who's sitting next to him. This guy, 50 Cent, undeniably has *it*—call it swagger, charisma, leadership, or circumstance, whatever it is that puts your name on everyone's lips. He's the biggest bad boy in the business at the moment and has made enemies with the most powerful drug dealers in New York.

That's just what Aftermath is interested in; they know their mostly white audience loves a gangster. But 50 Cent isn't the type of guy you want to negotiate a contract with. And the folks on the other side of the table aren't Dr. Dre; they are executives and lawyers who work at Universal Music Group, which owns Aftermath, and they are terrified.

The man at the table, 50 Cent, has recently recovered from being shot nine times. His previous label has dropped him. Everyone has had to drop him; after all, he is a marked man. As his producer Sha Money said, "Everybody was scared. Listen, someone came to assassinate him. What's stopping them from doing it again? It's a job that wasn't finished. You want to be there next to him the time that happens?" It's up to Lighty to convince these executives to take on that liability. All the swagger in the world won't close the deal—swagger won't be appropriate for the room. In this case, Lighty has to have something else: executive presence.

Danyel Smith, the former editor of *Billboard*, described Lighty: "His charm—man!—even (perhaps especially) for business meetings, he could turn it on. . . . Lighty was always reading situations. Anticipating. Strategizing. And then dinner was on him. If you were on his mental list of people whose calls he'd return, he was faithful and frank."

Aftermath signed 50 Cent, and the album that resulted, *Get Rich or Die Tryin'*, sold 14 million copies worldwide. 50 Cent became hugely famous and starred in a film named for the album. But that wasn't enough for Lighty. As digital music moved in, record sales weren't going to cut it anymore. Lighty believed "we have to constantly expand the opportunity and expand the realm of existence and opportunities for the artists. We can constantly push the envelope."[i]

He started getting endorsement deals off of the success of 50 Cent, most notably with Glaceau's Vitamin Water. Glaceau was still a start-up, and they couldn't afford an act as big as 50 Cent. Lighty convinced the founders to offer equity instead of cash. A few years later, Coca-Cola bought Glaceau for $4 billion and made Curtis Jackson, a.k.a. 50 Cent, a man who'd gotten his GED in a correctional facility, $100 million. All because of Chris Lighty's executive presence.

Many think this Vitamin Water deal changed music forever. When it occurred, the former business model of the music industry had already been destroyed by digital music, but it wasn't clear what was going to replace it—in particular, it wasn't clear how musicians were supposed to make money. And here, Lighty had made a rapper unimaginably rich. Lighty used their personalities and his presence to land artists big deals outside of record labels. It was a turning point that put artists in charge of their own careers and provided a model for how to be a successful artist in a post-label music industry.

Profile: Mary Barra

When Mary Barra became CEO of GM in 2014, she was the first woman in history to lead a major carmaker. But some would later speculate that instead of breaking the glass ceiling, GM had tried to push her off a glass cliff—they handed her the reins two weeks before a defect in the ignition systems of GM cars caused 124 deaths and one of the largest recalls in the history of the industry. But neither she nor her company would fall off that cliff. Instead, she embraced the crisis and used it to save the company from its own stagnant, siloed, and bureaucratic culture. In the same year, the company broke sales records despite the recall. Chairman of the board Tim Solso said, "She's done a superb job, and the board recognizes that."

Mary Barra's father was a diemaker who worked at the company for 36 years, and her modest but happy upbringing in the company town of Waterford, Michigan, can still be heard in the Midwestern lilt of her voice. Her first job at GM involved managing a mostly male, all-union maintenance team at Pontiac. When a bird flew into the factory, she had to address two problems at once: the bird, and the men who were competing with each other to kill the bird. She talked them down, lured the bird into a cage with some food, and released it near a lake.

When her plant closed down, she applied for a GM fellowship to get her MBA at Stanford University. After graduation, she returned to the company to work her way up the corporate ladder. She held a wide range of positions at the company, from product developer to head of human resources. In a move that would prefigure her leadership style, she whittled the company's 10-page dress code down to two words: "Dress appropriately." She showed her trust in the company's managers and workers to interpret that code and comply. Throughout her rise to the top, she earned the goodwill and respect of everyone in the company, both above and below her. In a forgivable lapse of his own executive presence, an anonymous GM senior staffer told *Time* magazine in 2014, "People were fucking elated when she got the job [of CEO]."

When the ignition defect scandal broke, she consistently struck the right tone in testifying before Congress and speaking to the press: She was genuinely contrite. She didn't downplay the harm the company had caused but made it clear that she was in control of the crisis. And she was. She told her employees, "I never want to put this behind us. I want to put this painful experience permanently in our collective memories." She eliminated layers of bureaucracy and empowered her employees to speak up and be heard. She told her executive management team, "We have 200,000 employees at General Motors—they want to do the right thing. Just make sure they know *you* want them to do the right thing."

The lessons of this trial by fire served Barra and GM well when the entire world faced a new crisis in 2020: the COVID-19 pandemic. GM was the first company to shift its focus from cars to masks and ventilators and successfully ran an on-site operation for this new manufacturing venture without increasing the exposure or risk for the employees who volunteered to participate. Barra continually uses crises to leverage and demonstrate GM's abilities as a competitive and nimble business. She says, "I have just seen so many things be done so quickly, without bureaucracy. The ventilator project: Literally, from when the first contact was made to when the first ventilator was rolling off the line, it was a month. I've already heard people in the company say, 'We want to go ventilator fast.' And I love that."

Profile: Dr. Renee Dua

Millions of brilliant and highly competent doctors work in the United States, but there is broad consensus that the medical profession as a whole is broken. In what is often seen as a stagnant and fractured system, nephrologist and internal medicine doctor Renee Dua has started a business that is revolutionizing how people receive medical care.

When Dua left medical school, she set up her own private practice. Building her own business and clientele took soft skills that they didn't teach in medical school. She recalls, "I would sit in the [doctors'] lounge and make friends. In medical school, you have a whole subset of doctors who do not come out with any bedside manner, let's be honest. So I had to learn how to be social, and fun, and make friends, and chew with my mouth closed, but build my business."

Meanwhile, she met her future husband, Nick, and they decided to have kids. After much difficulty getting pregnant, she gave birth to a son. He was admitted to the neonatal intensive care unit, so now she found herself on the other end of the care spectrum, as a mother.

Motherhood and medicine converged one Friday night when her son needed to go to the doctor. It was 5:00 p.m., and the doctor, in a hurry to leave, shooed them off to the ER. After hours spent waiting, they were seen by a resident, then a nurse, and finally the attending, who knew Dua. The attending asked, "What the hell are you doing here? You know this [stuff], right? You're a doctor." Dua was so beside herself, she said, "Look, I'm his mother, and this is nuts. How could you have made me wait so long? What are all the things that went wrong here?"

At that point Dua decided, "I want to stop being the kind of doctor I am and start doing house calls and just focus my attention on patients. What happened to me is not the kind of patient care I ever want to give anyone." In three weeks, Nick built an app, and they launched a medical practice called Heal. She started offering house calls around her community.

Together, the couple fundraised to scale their business and develop software for doctors to offer greater coordination and quality of care. In addition to house calls, they also used telemedicine and remote diagnostics and monitoring, so they were perfectly positioned to continue to provide quality care when COVID-19 struck in 2020. As their start-up gained attention, Lionel Richie became one of their earliest and most supportive investors.

As of this writing, Heal operates in eight states around the country, with a staff of 150 doctors and 50 support staff. Dr. Dua serves as the chief medical officer. She spends her time developing new software and products for doctors to build their own practices in their communities using Heal. And her success relies on her ability to communicate and make meaningful connections with people—just like she did back in medical school when she sat in the doctors' lounge making friends. She says, "To this day, if someone wants to work with us, the first person they talk to is me. That sounds silly, but it's because I speak the truth, and I'm not a salesman, and I want you to love working with us, so you might as well hear it from the horse's mouth first."

What Is Executive Presence?

These three people—Chris Lighty, Mary Barra, and Dr. Renee Dua—couldn't be less similar by almost any metric, other than their innovation and career success. All have exhibited executive presence in their own ways, putting their own slants on it and making something new of their very own. You can do it, too.

There are people in your life—they don't have to be the smartest people you know, but there is something about them that attracts you to them. You want to listen to them, learn from them, and perhaps allow their charisma to rub off on you. Those are people who have discovered and developed their own presence, perhaps even without meaning to. *Presence* here can be synonymous with charisma, swagger, magnetism, confidence—any number of qualities. But *executive presence* is much more specific; this is the type of charisma that will help you in your career, and as Lighty, Barra, and Dua have shown us, the way in which this charisma manifests can depend on the culture of your industry or your company. There is no one formula or prescription that will unlock it for you, but nonetheless it can be learned. In fact, it's not necessarily something that some people are just born with. It is a skill like any other, and this book will teach you how to acquire this valuable skill by giving you exercises and daily practices that will cultivate your executive presence.

Executive presence might seem like a slippery concept, because it's highly dependent upon the culture of your society, your company, and your industry. What is respected and appropriate in a recording studio will not work in a courtroom. This skill also requires the ability to change gears from situation to situation. Chris Lighty surely didn't behave in the same manner when he knocked on 50 Cent's door to sign him up and when he sat in the conference room with the execs at Universal Music.

Executive presence is rooted in others' perceptions of you as much as in your own actions, and that can make it feel out of your control. But it's not. CEO Bill, who dropped out of high school and worked parking cars at a country club, told me, "One of the men whose car I regularly parked told me if I'd stand up straighter, smile, and use 'yes, sir' and 'no, sir,' my tips would get bigger. And darned if he wasn't right. Everybody thought I had a Southern or military upbringing because of my respectful approach, but it was just me paying attention to the behavior I saw in people who seemed to be successful."

Bill founded his own international communications company focused on sports, so he loves a good sports metaphor. He explains, "Corporate America is like a football game. If you want to play the game you have to learn the rules, put on the uniform, go to practice, and try not to sit on the bench too long. You can't wear tennis clothes or bring a baseball bat to the football field because you love tennis and baseball. You have to know and play by the rules of the game you are in."

Despite the different rules for different environments, there are universal features of executive presence that can be learned and will work in nearly any situation. It is all about how you act and interact: in a memorable, impressive, credible, and genuine way. When you have this ability, you are comfortable in your own skin, with all the other Cs that matter—cool, calm, collected, curious, confident, and competent in your work. You're a contributor, a collaborator, and a communicator. Your civilized persona elicits a positive response from others, and your calculated, thoughtful actions help get useful things done.

As you consider the universal features of executive presence, you'll want to add your own slant to that definition. This is about being yourself. And being an observer. Intelligently watch what people do in different situations, particularly people you admire. Watch people who get positive reactions. Watch the pack—how do most people react in a given situation? In this case, it's not bad to do something a little bit different, a little extra, or a little more creative. Why? Because leaders stand out from the rest.

It's important to recognize that executive presence isn't achieved in a silo, nor is it used for recognition by a single group of people; executive presence transcends the boardroom. You take it with you into the cafeteria, the parking garage, and the community. Executive presence is the ability to inspire confidence in, generate trust with, resonate with, and impress:

- **Subordinates**, so they respect you and want to follow and emulate you.
- **Peers**, so they see you're capable and reliable and want to work with you.
- **Senior leaders**, so they see you have the potential for greatness.
- **Others you meet**, from the mailroom clerk to the security guard to the visiting job applicant, which will convey the sincerity in your presence.

Each chapter in this book explores a key quality you'll want to tailor to yourself in order to hone your executive presence. Each quality includes exercises and practical advice as well as suggestions for ways of thinking about these sometimes abstract concepts. From the lessons and philosophies in this book, you'll learn to improve your leadership, emotional intelligence, communication, comportment, and appearance, and you'll learn to do it all while still being authentically yourself.

Takeaways

- It's not enough to be smart, hardworking, and honest. Executive presence also involves setting yourself apart from all the other people who can say the same.
- How others perceive you is key. A favorable impression gets you noticed and remembered; you want to be hard to forget in a positive way.
- Executive presence is a skill that can be learned and that will help you thrive in your career, and it varies depending on the culture of your company or industry.
- Executive presence is not about an exaggerated sense of your own importance, and it is not a substitute for hard work and dedication. It requires authenticity.
- Executive presence transcends the boardroom. You take it wherever you go.

CHAPTER TWO

Leadership Styles

Executive presence is related to, but not the same as, leadership. Executive presence can help you become a leader, or it can help you become a better leader. You can be a leader without executive presence if circumstance puts you in charge of something—Mark Zuckerberg comes to mind. After all, he created Facebook in his dorm room, then dropped out of college to grow the company. However, for most people, you have to define what leadership means to you in order to define yourself as a leader.

In this chapter, we'll look at a variety of leadership styles, so you can see what you identify with and cultivate the leadership traits you want to manifest in yourself. As we explore the different leadership styles, we'll discuss what executive presence traits go well with them.

Executive presence gives you power, but it also gives you responsibility, and that's why you'll want to think about what kind of leader you want to be. We've already touched on how one leadership style doesn't fit every stage of growth, every industry, every culture, and every organization. While you may naturally possess traits of a particular leadership style, you can hone qualities found in other types of leadership to make yourself more agile. In one career, you may evolve from a visionary leader to a coaching leader, to a democratic leader, to a pace-setting leader, to a commanding leader, or any combination thereof—there's a time and place for all of it.

Visionary

A visionary leader sees the potential to change the world.

Modern visionaries such as Elon Musk, Jeff Bezos, and Mark Zuckerberg quickly come to mind. They are favorable toward innovation; *status quo* is a foreign term. They are intelligent risk takers, intensely focused, strategic, and resilient. This type of leader breaks away from what's comfortable or expected.

Jeff Bezos once said in an interview, "I'm willing to be misunderstood for a long time . . . until proven right."

No one can stop a truly innovative visionary. They are willing to take great risks. If you are risk-averse, this leader believes, nothing bad and nothing good may ever happen to you. Still, of course, risks can be taken too far.

Visionary leaders persist; they find creative ways around obstacles and are always looking for new opportunities. They envision what they want the future to look like, and then they organize and strategize to get there by laying out who should be doing what and when. Innovation is their driver. In the most collaborative manner possible, they will get people to buy into their vision through effective communication, emotional intelligence, optimism, and charisma.

This kind of leader is not afraid of failure, only of never trying. As one such leader put it, "The good thing about failing: It makes nobody jealous."

A typical visionary leader's self-image is charismatic and confident. This confidence affords them a sense of tenacity and determination, even and especially as they guide their organization through difficult times. Their charisma brings cohesiveness, inspiring everyone to be united in the vision. As big-picture people, visionaries do not bog themselves down with technical details, so they must rely on others to bring their vision to life.

Visionary leadership is especially important when:

- The company needs to create new leaders internally and/or fire up morale.
- Excitement must be generated within the company about the old mission.
- The company requires new innovation and a new direction to succeed, move to the next level, or surpass the competition.

Visionary leaders:

- Excite and inspire; people are drawn to their visionary thinking.
- Remain open-minded and willing to assimilate information from many sources to effectuate creative solutions.
- See the future as bright and problems as temporary.

Drawbacks to visionary leadership include:

- Although intelligent, they may lack empathy or emotional intelligence.
- Sometimes their futuristic, big-picture viewpoints overlook important details; they must hire detail-oriented people to work closely with them.
- Their futuristic orientation may cause them to miss the present moment and the opportunities within it.
- Their focus may make them inflexible, unwilling to change the plan or abandon it even when it doesn't make sense anymore. One visionary leader told me, "The facts may change, but my feelings still make me right."
- If they, as the owner of the vision, are absent, the organization can turn into a ship without a rudder unless they have carefully cultivated someone who understands the vision or has a contingency plan to step in.

- Because they are such a strong force, others in the organization sometimes take a back seat and abandon their own visions, deferring to their leader instead and thus potentially reducing morale.

Visionary leaders need to focus on the aspects of their presence that relate to their confidence and self-assuredness. They must project the courage of their convictions. As a visionary leader, you must:

- Be at ease and comfortable in your own skin.
- Not belong to anybody; belong to yourself.
- Take action when others don't. Do what's needed and let them help in whatever way is needed.
- Be dependable. Do what you say you will do. When things get tough, don't waver or quit.

Coaching

A coach helps their players be the best that they can be. Good coaches are always looking to bring out the best in their team, both as individuals and as a group. They use certain techniques that good teachers and good parents also use, including sending messages that guide and encourage rather than direct. For example, they are more likely to say, "Try this" than "do this."

This coaching style works as well for a business leader as it does for a sports coach. Instead of making all the decisions and delegating like an autocratic leader, a good coaching leader seeks to improve the performance and competencies of their employees by engaging them in two-way conversations, questions, and feedback. A good coaching leader promotes the responsibility and independence of the employees but still makes them feel supported in their work.

Doug Conant, former CEO of Campbell Soup Company, had a special onboarding process, as described by his employees. When Conant met a new subordinate, he invited them to a "full disclosure" conversation. He let them know how he likes to be communicated with (in person, by phone, online, etc.) and how he likes to receive good or bad news. In return, he invites the individual to explain how they prefer to communicate. Together, they come to an agreement that ensures optimum communication. By telling his employees how he works, he's giving guidance about how they can work.

A good coaching leader breathes new life into long-standing companies, as opposed to the visionary leader, who is better suited to giving birth to a new company.

The coaching leadership style inspires the team, builds their confidence as individuals, and gives them skills and encouragement to work together. Blame is replaced by constructive feedback and learning, and external motivators are replaced by self-motivation.

Coaching leaders:

- Encourage a sense of responsibility and commitment in employees.
- Encourage self-development of employees.
- Have a better idea of what is going on in the workplace because they are closer to the people.
- Reduce stress for workers and let them feel more in control.
- Reduce stress for the manager by providing guidance and assistance in leading the team.
- Cultivate a pipeline for advancement opportunities.

Drawbacks to coaching leadership:

- A hierarchical structure within most organizations can make it difficult to both coach and direct.
- The openness of these relationships may alter the level of professionalism by employees.
- If workers are unmotivated, they will not invest in self-development.

To be viewed as a coaching leader, it's necessary to:

- Hold no false pretenses. Be genuine.
- Be conversational and steady; don't dodge, spin, or whine. You're the leader and the rock.
- Listen and observe more than you speak.
- Be able to express yourself.
- Be helpful to others without worrying how it affects your job or stature.
- Be honest and establish a reputation as such.
- Give constructive feedback without criticizing or making someone defensive or uncomfortable.

Affiliative

An affiliative leader is typically well liked. This leader promotes harmony among the team and helps solve any conflict—their strategy for success is to strengthen the affiliations between all parties. They believe that the less conflict there is, the better the results will be. This leader focuses on creating personal connections between employees and their managers to build a sense of community and trust.

The affiliative leader might say, "Tell me where you want to go, and I'll take you there." This type of leader is most prevalent in nonprofits, community businesses, sports teams, and schools.

The affiliative leader seeks to understand others' needs to ensure their well-being and morale. This leader offers praise to motivate and encourage. They inspire people by making them feel like a part of the team.

Affiliative leaders might offer flexibility in working from home or casual Fridays to make for a more laid-back and comfortable work environment. These concessions are aimed at supporting the performance and morale of the team. Affiliative leaders are expert at creating positive emotional bonds with people, improving the communication process, encouraging reciprocity in positive behavior, and generating team spirit.

The affiliative leader might use simple questions to take the temperature of the team. Following are examples of such questions, as recommended by the UK-based marketing platform Success Factory:

- What was your best day at work in the last three months?
- What was your worst day in the last three months?
- What is the best manager relationship you've ever had?
- What's the best recognition you've ever gotten?
- When in your career have you learned the most?

The affiliative leader will take feedback from questions like these to guide them in leading as the people wish to be led versus how the leader themself might prefer to lead. It's imperative that this executive be genuine and credible in their efforts.

Affiliative leaders:

- Encourage creativity and innovative thinking so that teams share ideas more freely, without fear of criticism or judgment.
- Ease any emotional distress or fear of change in employees.
- Center on positive interactions; advocate for productive feedback and empathetic communication.

Drawbacks to affiliative leadership:

- It can create a sense of lacking leadership if the leader is too hands-off.
- An unrealistic expectation of constant harmony may surface, which can result in conflict-avoidant behavior.
- Employees' performance might decrease if they receive only positive feedback and never learn where to improve.

To be effective as an affiliative leader, it's necessary to:

- Have a kind disposition and express it through facial expressions, body language, words, and deeds.
- Listen and observe more than you speak.

Poor Leadership

I've never met a successful CEO who doesn't proclaim some version of "my people make the difference. They are most important to me." But sometimes, when I convey this message to their people, they say, "That's a surprise to us."

What some CEOs really mean by that is "for me to get the results I want, I need my people to make it happen because I can't do it alone." They are saying "my people are important" but what it really means is "my results are important."

In the past, leadership could pretty much be summarized as *command and control*. Like the old saying goes, the boss would say to jump, and you'd ask, "How high?" That directive doesn't work anymore. The autocratic leadership style of bygone days controlled all decisions and accepted very little input from others, internally or externally. These executives made choices based on their own experiences and beliefs, regardless of what was occurring in the economy or society, and they did not solicit suggestions or advice from others. Devoid of any collaboration or input, this operation in a silo was generally destructive and fostered the least creative workplaces imaginable. Perhaps your parents, but almost certainly your grandparents, worked under that kind of leadership.

The opposite extreme was the laissez-faire leader who relied entirely on their employees for direction and didn't really get involved in operations. This sort of structure worked only in situations involving team members whose skills were greater than the leader's. This type of leader avoids leading. You might find this lack of leadership in second-generation ownership of a company, in which the dad or mom built it and the son or daughter took it over because of family lineage but with little love for the business. In the Young Presidents' Organization, they call these reluctant second-generation leaders SOBs (sons of bosses).

Both autocratic and laissez-faire leaders may exhibit any of these traits:

- Inability to motivate a team
- Continually changing direction, appearing wishy-washy, and second-guessing decisions
- Poor communication
- Avoidant of conflict
- Self-centeredness or know-it-all behavior
- Rationalization of poor or unethical behavior
- Standing solidly behind whoever and whatever eventually wins
- Reserving the right to decide what is proper behavior
- Critical of others to make themselves feel important
- Inability or unwillingness to admit they are wrong (to themselves or others)
- Dishonest when they are pretty certain you'll never find out the truth
- Quick to see where others are wrong, but slow to see where others are right
- Disregarding of others
- Seemingly without conscience

Today, any type of leader can be a bad leader, but self-awareness can help anyone improve their leadership style. You are building this self-awareness by reading this book, taking a good look at yourself, and deciding how you want to lead.

However, even a bad leader can teach us something: what *not* to be.

Democratic

The democratic leadership style is based on mutual respect. It involves taking all opinions into consideration, making decisions with collaboration and input, and sharing responsibility equally. It's also referred to as participative leadership or shared leadership. It implies that the leader cares about their employees and considers them stakeholders.

Indra Nooyi, the former CEO of PepsiCo, is famous for reaching out to the families of employees with letters saying how proud they can be of their son, daughter, or partner; she even called the mother of an applicant who was undecided about joining the company.

Penn State University professor John Gastil defines democratic leadership as "distributing responsibility among the membership, empowering group members, and aiding the group's decision-making process."

A democratic leader places an emphasis on allowing broad participation during times of decision-making and problem-solving. Ideas are freely exchanged; discussion is encouraged. There tends to be more group equality, with a free flow of ideas, but the leader is still there to facilitate and offer guidance and ultimately has the final say in decisions.

Google founders Sergey Brin and Larry Page (both visionary leaders) recognized a need for democratic leadership in order to expand the company. They brought in CEO Eric Schmidt to jump-start a democratic leadership style at the company by setting up teams for product development.

The democratic leader generally possesses traits of honesty, intelligence, courage, creativity, competence, and fairness. This kind of leader has the ability to inspire trust and respect among followers.

Democratic leadership:

- Allows for considerable team engagement and participation.
- Encourages a creative environment.
- Increases connectivity between team members.
- Is applicable to nearly any business.

Drawbacks to democratic leadership:

- It can be more time-consuming than other types of leadership.
- With broad participation, processing decisions takes longer.

- It may introduce an element of uncertainty with regard to outcomes, as many ideas are considered.
- Once engaged in the process, people may feel resentful when their opinion doesn't carry the final decision.

A leader must be careful not to present a decision as one to be made democratically unless it is clearly possible. Democratic decisions cannot be made when the demands of the business or higher-ups have already cemented the decision. Be clear about what changes employees can give feedback on and the parameters within which employees may operate.

The executive presence of the democratic leader must portray a credible, genuine, trustworthy, competent individual, and one acting with considerable civility toward others.

To be effective as a democratic leader, it's necessary to:

- Speak directly and purposefully.
- Mean what you say and keep your promises.
- Be hopelessly honest—true to the core.
- Do what's right, even when it's not easy.

Pace-Setting

The term *pace-setting* comes from the person or thing that sets the pace for others to follow. This style often results in the most successful organizations because it focuses on meeting goals and maintaining a high-performing team. A pace-setting leader sets an example of high performance and a high pace and quality of work, and people are expected to follow suit. Although their expectations are great, this type of leader willingly assists with projects as necessary to ensure employees meet deadlines.

A pace-setting leader motivates their team with clear expectations of quality, service, and strict deadlines. You might hear a pace-setting leader use the expression "I don't suffer fools gladly," but ironically, they are pretty understanding when someone makes a mistake.

A famous pace-setting leader was Jack Welch, CEO of General Electric. He handsomely rewarded his top 20 percent of performers and fired the bottom 10 percent. This type of leader prioritizes performance over excuses and results over reasons.

One negative about pace-setting leaders is that they sometimes forget that they look good by making other people look good, not by making other people look bad. This phenomenon is often seen in accounting, law, and consulting firms, where hungry young recruits accept this leadership style and will work long hours to earn brownie points and get ahead of the competition (their own colleagues). They know if they do not, the pace-setting leader will quickly move on to someone else who meets the challenge.

If your attitude is "I need more time and I probably always will" or "I need to take breaks to do my best work," the pace-setting manager isn't a good match for you.

Pace-setting leadership:

- Clearly communicates the requirements to be met.
- Results in a high quality of output.
- Achieves business goals and swiftly addresses issues.
- Recognizes and leverages those individuals with the strongest competencies.

Drawbacks to pace-setting leadership:

- While the right result is expected, the *how?* is left to the individual, without clear guidance.
- Tasks cannot fall behind; things must get done quickly and correctly or those responsible are out.

- People can be easily overwhelmed with too much rigor.
- Leaders can become commanding (see next section) if they don't meet deadlines and desired levels of quality.

A pace-setting leader sets the pace, meaning that they must work harder than their employees. Nothing breeds resentment like being forced to meet unrealistic expectations while the boss takes long lunches and plays countless rounds of golf.

Commanding

Commanding leadership most closely resembles traditional autocratic leadership. Commanding leaders possess a natural take-charge attitude and are motivated to achieve. Generally, their attitude is "agree with me now, as it will save so much time." They tend to see things only from their own point of view.

Though they may have a handful of behind-the-scenes people whose input they trust and rely on, a commanding leader appears to make decisions alone and gives orders to people to meet goals and objectives. This leader moves quickly because they don't need to go through discussions to come up with a decision, which saves time. This is especially helpful during times of crisis.

You may see this in the military, where the leaders set direction for the mission, structure, actions, and well-being of their subordinates. Companies that are vendors to the military tend to adopt this style as well.

Interestingly, those who are commanding leaders in the office often behave the same way in their private lives. One such CEO came into a small western town and started buying up ranches set among the choicest scenery and hunting grounds that had been traditionally used by the locals for years. He used his money in a commanding fashion to cause locals to kowtow to him. It wasn't long before he was a persona non grata among the locals. You don't command cowboys, and he didn't realize that. He could have used executive presence, but he simply didn't care about approaching his new neighbors with any sort of finesse. He had money, he bought what he wanted, and everyone else was irrelevant.

The personality of the commanding leader is typically forceful, direct, and tough. Leaders with a commanding style are not afraid to make unpopular decisions and will take the helm to implement them. This leadership style may seem outdated for a modern leader, but there are still times, particularly during a crisis, when quick, decisive action is required, and a commanding leader is well suited to respond in this way.

In fact, humans respond well to a display of confidence. Executive presence requires that, and commanding leaders shine here. They speak firmly, and their audience responds by giving credibility and trust. The conviction of this leader makes them impressive and memorable; however, they could benefit from some of the affiliative leader's civility.

Commanding leadership is beneficial because:

- There is no ambiguity or uncertainty as to what is being asked.
- The gravitas of a commanding leader is useful and reassuring in times of crisis or chaos.
- Goals get met quickly, which is critical if decisions need to be made in order to save lives or instill order.

The drawbacks here are more pronounced than with other leadership styles. Commanding leaders:

- Provide little employee morale, as time is not taken to connect with people or keep them informed.
- Tend to manage by intimidation and steamroll people in the process.
- Cause stress and tension.
- May disempower and demoralize people who don't feel like they have a voice.

A commanding leader is successful only if their leadership style comes with executive presence. To be an effective commanding leader with executive presence, it's necessary to internalize these do's and don'ts:

- Don't be a sycophant, and don't tolerate sycophants. Be genuine in your dealings.
- Do express yourself clearly.
- Do help others without worrying about how it affects your job.
- Do establish a reputation of being honest so people continue to do business with you. This is equally important in a small town or major city.
- Do exude confidence—no one will follow you if you aren't confident.
- Do ignore when they like you and when they don't like you.
- Do understand that everyone around you will (both consciously and unconsciously) test your power and will.

Your Leadership Style (assessment)

Take a moment to consider your current beliefs.

- What do you think about your leadership style today?
- What factors contribute to you having that style?
- What style would you like to emulate?
- What leadership style does your manager have?
- What factors contribute to their style?
- What style would you like your manager to have?
- Who are the people who look up to you?

Now, assess your leadership style:

Visionary:

- Do you have ideas that you believe could change the world?
- Are you willing to take risks?
- Are you persistent and determined in your mission?
- Do you find your way around obstacles?
- Can you excite people to believe in your ideas?

Coaching:

- Do you strive to help people be the best they can be?
- Do you bring out the best in a team?
- Do you promote independence while still being part of a team?
- Do you listen more than you speak?
- Do you encourage a sense of responsibility in your people?

Affiliative:

- Do you like to promote harmony and minimize conflict?
- Can you build a sense of community among your people?
- Do you seek to understand others to better encourage and motivate them?
- Do you encourage and provide a comfortable workplace and style?
- Do you encourage team spirit, responsibility, and positive attitudes?

Democratic:

- Is your organization based on mutual respect and willingness to take in all opinions?
- Are decisions made with full team involvement?

- Do you encourage broad participation in problem-solving?
- Do you always strive for increased connectivity between people?
- Do you manage conflict with consideration of all involved?

Pace-Setting:

- Is meeting goals a main focus?
- Is maintaining a high-performing team another main focus?
- Do you set a high standard for quality of output for yourself?
- Do you communicate clear expectations?
- Do you quickly identify top performers?

Commanding:

- Are you a "take charge and follow my lead" type of person?
- Do you make decisions alone?
- Do you give orders and directions?
- Are you described as tough?
- Do you communicate firmly and clearly, without ambiguity?

Take a look at your "yes" answers in each category. You may see an overwhelming majority in one or two areas. You may even find you possess some traits in every style. This broad leadership capability can be most helpful, as different situations may call for different approaches. With the information you just collected, you can begin to tailor your personal brand of leadership.

Takeaways

- Today, more than ever, no one style fits all, and every leadership style has its benefits and drawbacks. A truly effective leader may naturally fit in one category but is skilled in tapping into other styles.
- Being flexible and utilizing the pros of all the styles does not make you inconsistent or unpredictable. It makes you adaptable, versatile, and open-minded.
- Whether you hit the right tone in leadership or not, enjoy the attempt and take pride in your willingness to take the lead. Leaders learn as much from failures as from their successes.
- The most challenging part of being a leader is understanding that you don't always know what's best for the team. In these situations, leadership styles that encourage teamwork and collective input can be vital.
- The surest way to become a bad leader is not to try. You're doing more than many others just by reading this book.

CHAPTER THREE

Emotional Intelligence

Intellectual intelligence will always be important; that's how you do your work, and it's certainly a prerequisite for leadership. But executive presence requires something rarer and more valuable: emotional intelligence.

Emotional intelligence is the awareness of and responsibility for the effect you have on others, as well as the empathy to acknowledge where others are coming from. It requires self-awareness, self-management, motivation, and social skills including empathy.

Emotional intelligence is a trademark of a good leader. This leader creates a more intuitive workplace for their people, putting their company a big step ahead of others. According to Barbara Bailey Reinhold, the author of *Toxic Work*, "When you don't listen to people and when you stay encased in your little capsule about data and forget about people, you cost the company a minimum of $750 a year per employee."

Self-Awareness

The first step of cultivating emotional intelligence is developing self-awareness. This includes the ability to identify your own thoughts and emotions and be thoughtful about where they come from, what triggers them, and what their impact is on others.

The more you know about yourself, the more readily you can choose the kind of person you can become. So ask yourself, what kind of person do you want to be? Increased self-awareness has a strong association with the Golden Rule: Treat others as you want to be treated.

The most successful type of self-awareness is twofold: internal and external. People who are internally self-aware understand their own character, feelings, core values, motives, needs, priorities, passions, habits, and desires. With that knowledge, they can follow their values, build on their strengths, and identify areas for improvement.

External self-awareness is the awareness that other people have their own characters, feelings, core values, motives, needs, priorities, passions, habits, and desires. That's where empathy comes from. This external self-awareness can help you see people for who they are and allow you to recognize how they see you. You won't always be right—you're not inside their heads—but empathy helps you understand where they are coming from and see yourself from their point of view more readily. External self-awareness, including empathy, helps you ensure that the message you send is received as you intended.

Sometimes, however, self-awareness can turn into self-criticism. It's important to be aware of this, because if you put yourself down, others will also. A later self-assessment will help clarify those boundaries.

Too often, areas of life such as religion, parenting, and coaching teach us to put ourselves down. The healthiest approach to these messages is to be aware of your imperfections while accepting them and know that they don't define you. You are deserving of acceptance and kindness from others and from yourself. You are adequate and good enough. That might not sound like a high standard to meet, but too many of us believe we're inadequate—a lie that culture or our families or our bosses might have implanted in us. Some call it *imposter syndrome*. If you don't alter your thinking to dismiss this imposter, you'll create an unnecessary obstacle for your executive presence.

One CEO I know said, "It all comes down to your own self-belief. If you believe you're okay, one day you'll wake up and find you truly are. . . . If you don't believe in yourself, you better know that no one else will. You haven't got a hope in hell."

Similarly, as you reach out to learn from and connect with people, view them as at least adequate, too. Assume good intentions and high ability in others. If you talk to a stranger a day, but then each day find yourself thinking critically, negatively, or judgmentally about that person, you are not setting yourself up to manifest executive presence. The person working toward executive presence is slow to judge and treats people like they themself want to be treated.

An amateur leader thinks that people are like them. A pro knows and accepts the differences, acknowledges another person's right to think differently, and embraces the possibilities such diversity of thinking might generate.

To practice acceptance requires a shift. Imagine an employee is spending inordinate time chatting at the watercooler when a deadline is looming. Instead of thinking that person is a jerk, dumb, or slacking off, think about something the person does well and focus on that. Then, if you are their manager, give clear direction as to what you want and don't want in their behavior without judging their character, motive, or ability. With this shift in perspective, you can constructively address behavior that is not what is expected without attacking the person's character.

I learned this belief from some of the greatest leaders in the world and have maintained it for many years: As a leader, your job is to do yours while doing all you can to maintain the self-esteem of others. The leader who can be proudest of their leadership is one who never compromises the dignity of another person.

Emotional Intelligence Self-Assessment

Check off any of the following statements that apply to you:

- ☐ I am curious about people and what makes them tick.
- ☐ I know my strengths and weaknesses.
- ☐ I look for the strengths in others.
- ☐ I accept others' character, good intentions, and abilities even if I perceive a weakness.
- ☐ I understand what leadership style I respond to most favorably and why.
- ☐ I don't think I am smarter than others.
- ☐ I try to make people feel safe to take risks.
- ☐ I allow others to make mistakes and learn from them.
- ☐ I affirm other people often, through compliments or pointing out when they do something well.
- ☐ I empower people to make decisions.
- ☐ I'm unafraid to ask opinions about an area of expertise outside of my own.
- ☐ I publicly acknowledge good work from peers.
- ☐ I am a good listener.
- ☐ I motivate people to do things they wouldn't have done if I had not been there.
- ☐ I embrace change.
- ☐ I consider myself a good judge of character.
- ☐ I stop myself from negative self-talk and negative thoughts toward others.
- ☐ I can disconnect from uncomfortable situations when I want to.
- ☐ I am difficult to offend; I don't hold grudges.
- ☐ I appreciate what I have.

- ☐ I know when to say no to myself and others.
- ☐ I don't expect perfection from myself or others.
- ☐ I can neutralize toxic people.

Self-Awareness Exercise: Autobiography

Take some time, even a few hours, to write your autobiography. Write about where you grew up, the kind of work your parents did, your influences along the way, experiences that shaped you, and coaches or teachers or others who guided you as well as why you chose to go to the college you did, study the subject you did, and join the company you did. Write where you met your partner (or how you lost your partner), what you do for fun as an adult, what makes you happy, who makes you happy, what makes you unhappy, who makes you unhappy, and what you see for your future. Include any other stories or details that resonate for you.

By writing your life story, you:

- Can reflect with pride on what you've become or see what you still need to do to become who you want to be.
- Identify your strengths and weaknesses and understand what to enhance and what to build on.
- Organize your history so you can talk about yourself in a job interview or presentation and tell stories of your history and accomplishments as examples, rather than claims and platitudes.
- Can share it with your children or loved ones so they know more about you and your history.

Self-Awareness Exercise: Emotional Awareness

1. Take a moment to sit quietly and reflect. Think of a personal or workplace experience or situation in which you felt:
   » calm
   » irritated
   » excited
   » worried

2. Think about what triggered those feelings.
3. If it was a positive feeling, consider how you can replicate those feelings. For example, if you were calmed by the words of your boss, you might take notes as to what they said that was so impactful and compose something similar to use in the future to calm yourself and/or those you lead.
4. If it was a negative feeling, consider what you can do about it going forward. For example, if you always worry in the weeks leading to your performance review that you won't express yourself effectively, you might consider asking your boss to receive a copy of the review before the meeting so you have time to digest the information beforehand in order to formulate a response.

In this exercise, the first step is recognizing, then thinking, then changing behavior. Even if it's just a trial run, change a behavior to see how it feels.

This may feel uncomfortable at first, especially if you are not normally introspective. However, these are private, internal conversations you are having with yourself, so you can be honest. Get a journal and write down your thoughts.

Self-Management/Regulation

Self-management is also called self-control; simply put, it's the ability to keep your emotions in check so you can be intentional about your interactions and behave effectively and appropriately in different situations.

When you reign over yourself, even with regard to your passions, desires, and fears, you master self-management. Without self-restraint, life is spent fighting difficulties of one's own making. Every temptation to judge, every negative perspective, every poorly chosen word said or typed diminishes power and effectiveness. When this happens, others who aren't as talented but have self-control will prevail.

A person who can't manage themself has little hope of managing others or leading a team. Moments of self-control in escalated situations will determine your destiny. For example, if a person loses their temper, they lose control of the situation. If you stop doing the right thing for even a moment, that moment can have a negative effect for days, months, even years. It's like driving, where a second or two with your eyes diverted to a text can cause an accident with lasting repercussions. The opposite occurs when you do the right thing for even one or two seconds. Rosa Parks made a decision to remain seated and changed history forever.

Staying in control involves managing your mindset but also your countenance, tone of voice, body language, gestures, and words.

If self-control is something you struggle with, you can work on this through self-awareness. By learning what triggers you and how to manage the emotions that are triggered, you will become more persistent, resilient, patient, perceptive, and self-confident. As an employee with good self-control, you will be more productive, dependable, and able to manage your career path and set an example for others. As a person, you will feel more at ease with yourself.

Self-management is as much about how you do your work as it is about your work itself. You're intelligent, and you've got the skills, but others do, too. The tiebreakers here are your emotional intelligence and self-management: Can you deal with people with kindness and poise and do your work with grace?

I tell clients, regardless of their job title, "You are the CEO of your own life, and your own personal board of directors!" You can be the kind of boss you would like to have. You are in charge of your attitude, your behaviors, your interactions, and your reactions.

If you start with self-awareness, you can determine where you are and what you want to be and use self-management techniques to ensure that your behavior will get you there. If you look at it through this lens, no one and nothing can take you down. You "fly the plane" or "ride the dragon," as a colleague put it.

Self-Management/ Regulation Assessment

It is a good start to believe that you are in control of your thoughts and actions. The real test is whether others experience you the way you want them to. Your intent is the starting point, but the effect you have on a given situation is the result.

Self-assessment and self-reflection can be done anywhere and under any circumstances. But you can't count on pressure from your peers to make you do it. It's your time, in your mind. It's up to you to monitor your own learning progress and performance, just as you are responsible for being aware of your strengths and weaknesses. Far better for you to know them yourself than to let others discover them!

In this exercise, you'll write (or reflect on) the story of your career to this moment. Focus on your accomplishments so that at the end you will be able to discern a list of your top achievements. Review each achievement and evaluate:

- Was it self-motivated or other-motivated?
- Did it come from a skill that was self-taught or taught to you by others?
- Was it an independent activity, or did you act as part of a team?
- What motivated this accomplishment? Money, power, reputation, the work itself, or something else?
- Was it a public accomplishment or private victory?
- How did you resolve any struggles that arose along the way?
- How did you communicate during the process?
- What did you find attractive about the work?

Next, look for patterns across events. Maybe you see a trend that you are a team player, maybe a lone ranger; perhaps you're attracted to numbers versus aesthetics; you're a hell-raiser or peacemaker, a politician or limelight avoider. When you see a pattern, if you like it, develop it. If you see a pattern of behavior that you don't want to continue, pinpoint that as a goal to work on and change.

Years ago, I performed a self-assessment like this, and I learned so much about myself, including that:

- I needed to be my own boss.
- I would not make a good employee because I wanted to run the show. (I didn't like being told what to do or how to do something. I wanted to try it myself and see if it worked, and if it didn't, I was willing to try again until it did.)
- I like to work on my own.
- I like to learn from others, listening and watching those I admire.

What have you learned about who you are, how you work, and how you can use that information to grow and change?

Self-Management/ Regulation Assessment:

1. Set a goal to improve in an area in which you need more self-management. For example, maybe you speak out too quickly and have a tendency to tell other people what to do.

2. Write down what you think it will take to achieve that goal. For example, instead of speaking over people, you could:
   » Bite your tongue and refrain from speaking.
   » Write it down so you don't forget it if you decide you want to say it later.
   » Listen to what others are saying about it, and write down your thoughts. Later, you can reflect on your thoughts and the thoughts of others and see if a better solution comes from the diversity of ideas.
   » Ask a question to learn more about the subject: "Can you tell us more about _____? Have they tried _____? When does this have to happen? What happens if nothing is done?"

3. Follow through. Really, truly refrain the next time the situation arises, on the phone or in person. Do not allow yourself to speak first or early on.

4. Review what happened. After the moment passes, think about the outcome since you didn't speak up. If you need to, follow up with the person and communicate any outstanding thoughts.

5. Analyze what you could have done differently to improve next time. If you did speak up too soon because you just couldn't hold yourself back, weigh whether what you said

actually added value, and think about what might have happened if you hadn't spoken so quickly.

6. Get feedback on how it affected others, either directly (e.g., "Do you feel the outcome was better because we handled the conversation like we did?") or indirectly, by just observing the reactions, motivation, and morale of people involved.

7. Embrace what is working fast, and get rid of what's not working faster. If you held back once today, try again tomorrow and the next day. After a while, the action (or inaction) will become your default approach. In the example provided here, you let others look smart and maintain their self-esteem and took pressure off yourself to perform. The takeaway in this example: Never be lax in contributing, but wait until after you hear others, so you can add, "That's a great idea! And I was thinking, would _____ help, too?"

8. Put this exercise aside for a month and then revisit it based on changes you've made. It wouldn't be worth doing if it were easy, but it is very rewarding and has lasting effects. Take pride in how you manage yourself.

Self-Management/ Regulation Exercise: Talk to Others

For the next week, try to talk to someone new every day—this can be someone you already know. While you're at it, see if the opportunity presents itself to ask one of these questions about others' self-management techniques. You may pick up some helpful tips:

- How do you stay focused?
- How do you motivate others?
- How do you manage your time?
- How do you sell your ideas and influence people?
- How do you deal with difficult people?
- How do you make decisions?
- How do you stay calm?

When you ask your question, simply listen. You may wish to follow their answer with, "Can you give me an example?"

Self-Management/Regulation Exercise: Deep Breathing

Health experts say that deep breathing has many benefits: It improves blood flow, releases toxins from your body, helps you sleep better, improves immunity, and works as a natural painkiller. Of course, the greatest benefit is that it reduces anxiety.

To practice helpful deep breathing:

1. Breathe in through your nose for a count of four. Let your belly fill with air.
2. Breathe out through your nose for a count of four (or your mouth if that is more comfortable).
3. Place one hand on your belly. As you breathe, feel it rise.
4. Take three more deep breaths.

This kind of deep breathing is widely practiced to foster calm and control in every situation, including by Navy SEALs.

On Intelligence Alone

A private equity firm contacted me to ask if I would work with one of their rising stars. His manager explained, "He's off-the-charts bright, but he needs to step up to the bat and take control of the power that can be his. He's the smartest man in the room, but he doesn't speak up, and when he does, he's very dogmatic. Two other things: He has gained some weight from all the work travel, and his shirt is tight across his belly. I don't think he can even button his jacket. And when he eats, he slops his food all over his clothes and sometimes others, too. All of this is too delicate to discuss with him; in fact, I'm afraid I could get into legal trouble approaching him about this. That's why we need you to talk to him. Oh, and make sure he doesn't know that I told you any of this."

First, we ate a meal together so I could see for myself his poor manners. Then I got him talking about his background, skills, strengths, and weaknesses. We talked about what was frustrating him in his career. He told me he was valedictorian of his high school and carried a 4.0 GPA at Northwestern. He had started out of college along with some peers who were similarly experienced, intelligent, and ambitious. He explained, "Today, three of those guys have bigger titles and make more money than I do. We all started out the same, but something caused them to excel and me to be stuck."

We discussed executive presence and how he could retain individuality but be more effective in managing up, sideways, and down. I got him to accept the simple idea of buying larger shirts that covered his belly until he could lose the weight. We explored how he could communicate in a more empathetic way and still get results. I also worked with him on speaking up more often to test ideas.

Later, his boss told me, "I would have paid you three times what I did for the changes you've helped him make."

continued

He did well for a couple years, using all the tools of executive presence consistently, and it allowed his intellectual strength to shine through. Over time, as he received more and more accolades for his intellectual attention, he grew arrogant and forgot to consciously work on the emotional intelligence tools we had worked on together. He began to lose trust and angered his coworkers.

Executive presence is a package deal—there are many facets, and they all require continuous intentionality. Don't lose sight!

Motivation

Motivation is your enthusiasm to do something. It's your choice, and you are the only one who can control it. You can have intrinsic motivation or extrinsic motivation. The former comes from within yourself, much like inspiration, and the latter comes from either a reward you will earn for good performance or a punishment you will suffer for bad performance. Intrinsic motivation can be sparked by an immediate opportunity or idea, or it can be a general quality that pushes us to do well in life. Intrinsic motivation is also usually more powerful, but like the old concept of the carrot and the stick, we all know that rewards and punishments can be extremely useful in certain situations.

If you're highly intrinsically motivated, you likely:

- Did well in school.
- Have a good sense of self-awareness.
- Have good self-management and self-control.
- Habitually set goals.
- Seek continuous advancement.

This kind of motivation can keep you succeeding and achieving, but for some, it's sort of a never-ending, never-fulfilled state. Those folks climb the mountain because it's there, not to see what's on top.

Motivation comes in many forms. A CEO I know who was dealing with liver disease brought on by excessive drinking told me this story: "I was in the hospital, at death's door, and I thought I saw the devil come to me and say, 'You remind me too much of myself—get out of here.' A nurse was sitting up with me late that night and I said, 'What's going on?' She said, 'They have a pool going to see if you're going to make it.' That's all I needed to hear. I got up out of that bed and started walking my ass off." That's motivation.

Without motivation in some area, you can't achieve anything. You have no purpose. With motivation, you persist longer, produce higher-quality effort, and perform better. To discover your own motivation, go back to the self-management/regulation assessment (page 42) and look at your accomplishments again. Think back to what motivated you at the time. Was it peer pressure, money, or the desire to please a parent or professor, to beat someone else at the game, to elevate the team, to improve your reputation, to repair your reputation, to get someone's attention, to avoid a penalty or punishment, or just to get it done and get out of there?

That's where you've been. Now, see where you want to go. Reflect on these two questions:

1. When you add to your life story in three to five years (which you should), what do you want to have done? What do you want to be known as? What skills do you want to possess? What will be your personal brand? How will you be making an impact? What would you love to be doing?

2. If money weren't an issue, what would you change about your previous answers?

Now, think about what it will take to make that story happen.

Motivation Self-Assessment

Take out your journal, and as you write, ask yourself:

- What is going great in my life?
- What are my top three goals?
- What beliefs or fears are holding me back?
- Why is now the best time to take action? If not, why not?
- What will motivate me to start, continue, and not stop?
- What is my desired outcome?

Answer these questions, then tell yourself what you can do at this point in time to make things happen.

No one can motivate you like you can yourself, but sometimes it helps to pause and really consider what causes you to make the decisions you do. Thinking about what you want to achieve is the first step; doing something about it is the separating factor.

Motivation Exercise: Understand Others' Motivations

Turn to someone else, and ask them questions about their motivations. You can choose a colleague, a friend or a family member, or a stranger. After you actively listen to their responses, consider how their responses are similar to and different from the ones you would give.

Questions you can ask:

- How did you find your career path or your passion?
- What gave you confidence to pursue your path?
- What got you the job you are in?
- What do you think were (or are) your competitive advantages—the separating skills?
- How did (or do) you differentiate yourself?
- What are the boldest things you've done to set yourself apart?
- What setbacks have you had? How did you deal with them?
- What do you take pride in?
- What do you fear?
- What have you sacrificed?
- What do you long for?
- Who were/are your role models?
- What was the single smartest thing you did to advance your career?
- What was the most surprising method to achieve success in your career?
- What were your missed opportunities—your biggest regrets?
- How have you been tested the most?
- What do you wish others knew about you?

You might not be able to ask one person all of these questions. For better insight, focus on getting folks talking, rather than running down the list.

Motivation Exercise: Talk About It

It's helpful to understand and use your own motivation as a driver. In the process, it's important not to judge others' motivations. Their lives are theirs to live. That said, it can be insightful to understand why a coworker is making a certain decision or going in a particular direction. Instead of guessing why, ask why.

You can say, "You've clearly put a lot of thought into the direction you are going. Do you mind telling me your thinking behind it?" Then quietly listen as they speak. No matter how brief or lengthy the answer, ask a few more follow-up questions so you fully understand.

This skill comes with many benefits:

- By asking instead of judging, you allow others to maintain their self-esteem.
- You'll learn what line of thinking was behind the decision, which may help you work with what was decided.
- You'll be perceived as an open and nonjudgmental listener—a valuable quality in dealing with coworkers at all levels.
- By considering others' motivations, you get insight into your own motivations.

Empathy

Empathy is the ability to relate to other people's emotions and imagine what they might be thinking or feeling. It's the closest you can get to being in their shoes. Empathy is always remembering that you are not the only one with thoughts and feelings.

Empathy sounds similar to sympathy, but with sympathy, you are feeling sorry for the person; with empathy, you are imagining their situation without judging it.

One CEO explains business success as "sensitivity to other people's reactions, appreciation of human values, creative imagination, reliability, physical ruggedness, financial gusto, and the ability to be right 95 percent of the time—but especially sensitivity to other people's reactions and knowing what to do about it."

We've talked about respect and the act of choosing to respect others' characters, motives, and abilities, even when they differ from our own beliefs. That is a big part of empathy: understanding the perspectives, experiences, and motivations of another individual. An empathetic person accepts that we're all different, but we all have value.

People with empathy:

- Act, look, and sound like they really care.
- Understand that sometimes it's best not to try to solve others' problems or dispense advice, but rather to listen to their perspective.
- Don't dismiss another person's feelings.

Part of executive presence is being able to relate to people who aren't like yourself. A leader with executive presence will show empathy when they see:

- A person being bullied.
- An overwhelmed coworker.
- A person having a bad day.
- An individual, even one with competing interests, in emotional or physical pain.
- An individual dealing with a marital breakup or the loss of a family member.

Growing up in an environment that teaches empathy is a likely precursor to having empathy as an adult. But even if empathy was not a part of your upbringing, as a thinking adult, you can always develop and improve your level of empathy. It can actually be beneficial to read biographies and novels, because as the reader you are drawn into the perspective of the protagonist or the related characters. By stepping into the alternate reality that a book provides, you see how others' minds work in ways that you would normally not have access to. You discover what drives them and their reactions and decisions.

Another easy way to develop empathy is to simply listen. Make an effort to be alert and ready to listen to how other people express what they are thinking and feeling. Pay attention. We all know how to look like we are listening, but to show you're truly listening, you'll want to:

- Turn off outside distractions; put down phones and tablets.
- Put aside your own thoughts and opinions.
- Carefully think about what the other person is saying.
- Don't champ at the bit for them to finish just so you can jump in.
- Resist the urge to interrupt.
- When they finish speaking, encourage them to build on what they said, such as, "Tell me more about _____."

Be patient, attentive, and open to differing opinions. You may learn something that changes your mind, and, more importantly, you will make the person feel heard. You will allow them to maintain their self-esteem through your acceptance of their different experiences, motivation, accomplishments, etc. And if they feel heard by you, they will more likely hear you in return, and certainly they will appreciate you for your empathy.

Empathy is an emotional connection that adds to your executive presence. Your empathetic actions can be more effective even than the words you choose or your overall behavior. Without it, an effort is hollow, but with it, trust is developed.

Narcissistic, schizoid, antisocial, and selfish people often lack empathy, but this is not for us to judge. It's not empathetic to criticize them. Instead, we should try to understand why they are the way they are and determine how we can find common ground with them.

People with other conditions, such as autism spectrum disorder, are often seen as lacking empathy, but that suggestion might come as a surprise (or an incongruity) to the person with autism. People with autism feel emotions as strongly as (or more so than) anyone else but might have trouble expressing them. This is another reason not to negatively judge someone you perceive as lacking empathy, even while you strive to cultivate it in yourself.

As a manager, you must never let a non-empathetic person cause you not to do your work well. Instead, as a leader, you can accept that there are people like that and determine you will not be one yourself.

Empathy Self-Assessment

Check off the statements that apply to you:

- ☐ In conversation, when the other person is talking, I'm busy thinking of what I'm going to say next.
- ☐ I'm often awkward or don't know what to do in a social situation.
- ☐ I'm often confused or taken by surprise when someone tells me they are offended by something I said.
- ☐ I enjoy being the center of attention at a party.
- ☐ If someone asked me what I think of their new haircut, I would give them my honest opinion even if I don't like it.
- ☐ I always check the news, no matter how bad; I think it's important not to look away from suffering.
- ☐ I've been told I'm intruding in a situation and been surprised to hear that.
- ☐ People have told me that I go too far with jokes or teasing people.
- ☐ I don't think it's a big deal if I'm late for an engagement.

This assessment is intended to give you a baseline of your empathy, not to judge it. Although a high number of checked items is associated with decreased empathy, there's nothing really wrong with liking to be the center of attention at a party or being awkward. Practice self-compassion as you learn about yourself and how you can grow stronger in this area.

Empathy Exercise: Reframe Conflict

Select someone who causes you problems in life or at work. Ask yourself these questions:

- What do I need to learn about this person?
- What would be useful to know about this person?
- What would be fun to know about this person?
- How can I use that information to improve my working relationship with that person?

Now ask yourself:

- What do I wish people knew about me?
- What would be useful for them to know?
- What would be fun for them to know?
- How could they use that information to improve their working relationship with me?

Simply pausing to think and consider these questions can provide some level-headedness, as you consider that person on a more human level, and can help you better deal with challenging interpersonal situations.

Empathy Exercise: Interaction Debrief

Think of a conversation that you're going to have soon that you're feeling apprehensive about. What is the fear?

After you have the conversation, ask yourself a few questions about how it went:

1. Did I consider their feelings when I was expressing my opinion?
2. Did I consider their point of view?
3. Did I ask what they thought before I said what I thought?
4. Did I listen without judging?
5. Did I refrain from interrupting?
6. Did I ask more about the situation so that I fully understood their perspective?

Don't be hard on yourself if you did only a few of these things, but in the next conversation, strive for 4, 5, and 6.

Social Skills

In this chapter we've looked at necessary attitudes for executive presence: self-awareness, self-management, motivation, and empathy. The practical, applied uses of these skills are your social skills, which help you get along sooner and better with others; they enable you to create and maintain satisfying relationships.

Social skills include:

- Manners
- How you communicate

- The consideration you show others
- How you express your own personal needs

Your upbringing introduced you to these social skills, and regardless of the extent that they were ingrained in you, as an adult, you can choose to enhance and develop them.

When you are armed with social skills:

- People tend to gravitate toward you.
- Making friends and getting supporters and followers comes more easily.
- You are more comfortable initiating social contact.
- You laugh more readily, including at yourself.
- You cooperate and collaborate more often.
- Your daily vernacular includes phrases like "please" and "thank you."

If you have self-awareness, self-management, motivation, and empathy but do not apply those attributes to your social skills, you will tend to experience more stress and loneliness.

Chris Segrin, researcher and head of the University of Arizona Department of Communication, writes, "We've known for a long time that social skills are associated with mental health problems like depression and anxiety. But we've not known definitely that social skills were also predictive of poorer physical health. Two variables—loneliness and stress—appear to be the glue that binds poor social skills to health. . . . The use of technology—texting, in particular—is probably one of the biggest impediments to developing social skills in young people today. Everything is so condensed and parsed out in sound bites, and that's not the way that human beings for thousands of years have communicated. It makes young people more timid when they're face-to-face with others, and they're not sure what to say or what to do. There's no social interaction, and I fear that's really hurting people."

It's hard to deny the impact that technology and texting are having on young people's ability to communicate on a professional level, and experts seem to agree that the ability to communicate effectively will play a large deciding role in their likelihood to succeed and the degree of their success.

Social Skills Self-Assessment

Check all that apply to you:

- ☐ I believe that people feel comfortable around me.
- ☐ I can defuse a tense situation without conflict.
- ☐ I don't have to worry that I might say something insensitive, because I'm not thinking anything hurtful.
- ☐ I like to dress up and wear a suit or even a tux or gown.
- ☐ I'd rather be overdressed than underdressed.
- ☐ I am sensitive to what is considered polite in other cultures and can modify my own behavior as appropriate.
- ☐ I make friends easily.
- ☐ I don't avoid conflict when necessary, because I know how to frame issues in a positive and constructive manner.
- ☐ I like to watch English period piece dramas of manners.
- ☐ I value being a member of a society perhaps even more than I value my individuality.
- ☐ I don't play a character or wear a mask in social inter-actions. I am me.
- ☐ I usually give people the benefit of the doubt.

If you've checked off many boxes, your social skills are likely quite strong. However, the absence of check marks in certain areas is not indicative of a lack of social skills. Not everyone with social skills likes to dress up, nor do all enjoy English period pieces on manners. This activity simply highlights the areas of social skills in which you excel.

Social Skills Exercise: Improve Your Social Skills

1. Observe what is going on around you with people in your family, at work, or at the grocery store.
2. When you notice something—for example, someone cuts in line in front of another person at the store, or snaps at the deli manager for being slow, or drops an item off the shelf and lets it sit there where someone could trip on it, think about how this scene looks to others. Think about when you might have done something similar. Think about what you will do next time when you catch yourself being less than thoughtful.
3. If there is something you can do to make up for these social skills infractions, show compassion by doing so. Compliment the deli manager (or at least express understanding if service is slow), pick up the item that fell on the floor, make sure not to cut in front of someone, or, if they have fewer items, invite them to step in front of you.

Thinking about a situation, then acting on your thoughts, sets you apart from others who don't think but only react. Those with good social skills act and react with self-awareness and self-management.

Social Skills Exercise: Track Yourself

This exercise will simply require you to keep track of how often you say "please" and "thank you." Every time you say one of those words, give yourself a mental check mark. Likewise, every time someone says one of those words to you, make a mental note of it.

Keep this up for a few days and try to increase the number of times you use the words. Note the responses and reactions you get from others. Also, keep track of how often others say it to you. Pay attention to how it feels. Be careful to avoid judgment that someone should have said one of those words more often. Just make note of the effect it has on you when you receive these expressions and when you don't.

Takeaways

- There are off-the-charts bright people who have a lot of work to do to gain executive presence. Intellectual intelligence is necessary but not sufficient.
- The more you know about yourself, the more easily you can choose the kind of person you want to be.
- We are all adequate. We come into adulthood the way we were raised. But although we cannot change the beginning, we can change the present and the future.
- You are the CEO of your own life. As a capable adult, you can be whatever you want to be and learn all the skills in this book.
- Moments of self-control in escalated situations will determine your destiny. You're in charge of your attitude, behaviors, and reactions.
- People want to be respected. Give respect and acceptance.

CHAPTER FOUR

Communication

All day, every day, you are communicating. Generally speaking, you can't communicate too much; it seldom makes anything worse. If you keep at it, clear communication will eventually improve just about any situation. However, saying nothing doesn't mean you're not communicating anything. All day, every day, we are all transmitting messages. The question is whether your message is the one you intend to send.

With executive presence, communication is more than the words you say or type. It's your tone when sending a message that calms or grates and the use of storytelling that helps you be better understood as well as remembered and repeated.

Communicating with executive presence shows you are a professional; in doing so, you can build and improve relationships, manage conflict, and successfully navigate difficult conversations.

Tone

Tone is dependent on self-awareness. If you aren't aware of your own feelings, you may be surprised by how people act when you speak to them; statements that you thought were neutral might be perceived as aggressive, perhaps because you're not aware of your tone or simply because you're stressed.

Tone denotes the tonality of your voice, your choice of words, the pace and volume at which the words are spoken, and even the speed of your response to a statement, text, or email. *Tone* incorporates words, facial expressions, and attitude. It's not about just what you say but also how you say it and the impression and impact it has on your audience. It's the expression of your meaning behind the words, as perceived by others.

Say you are having dinner and the phone rings. You decide to answer. If the call is from a solicitor, your tone of voice will be measurably different than if the call is from a college friend you had lost track of and have been wondering about. Your tone would be entirely different if the caller were a family member telling you urgent news. We all use varying tones depending on the conversation subject, our attitude at the time, how alert we are, and even how we are feeling physically.

Tone can either clarify or confuse your meaning. For example, if you say something but end it with uptalk, meaning you raise your voice at the end of a sentence, it may be perceived as a question. Uptalk does not convey confidence, nor does it generate confidence in those listening to you.

A voice quality that works well in executive presence is one I call a "pass the salt" tone of voice. Even if you are mad or agitated, you don't yell, "Pass the salt." You make the request in an even, neutral tone. We can also call it a boardroom voice. This, again, involves speaking in an even and consistent timbre. That said, *boardroom* is not to be confused with *bored room*—a monotonous tone that drones on and sends a totally different message. The boardroom tone is loud enough to hear without straining, at a pace that isn't too fast or too slow, and accompanied by a facial expression and body language that are consistent with the message. It is not too brassy, ringy, breathy, sweet, whispery, or dull but rather respectful, enthusiastic, and thoughtfully chosen.

Tone is a powerful thing—it communicates your feelings even more powerfully than words. People respond to tone. To picture this, think of tonality like energy. Physical energy is required to use your diaphragm and vocal cords to project words out of your mouth. Intellectual energy is needed to ensure the correct meanings of the words coming out of your mouth. And finally, emotional energy is tapped into to create the desired inflection.

The tone or spirit of your words can come across in written form as well. Using all capital letters in a text is widely regarded as yelling, as is the use of a red typeface or curtness. They all send a message.

As it relates to executive presence, a big part of a successful tone in voice and attitude is the self-confidence it portrays. A later exercise shows you how you can use your range of tones to send different messages.

To display confidence in your tone:

- Speak with simplicity and clarity.
- Slow down your speaking.
- Project a bit bigger.
- Use the boardroom tone, regardless of the emotional content, but sprinkle in some variety: Emphasize key parts of your message with a few words that are quieter, bigger, a little faster, or a little slower. Think of it like music, which varies in cadence and scale to resonate with the listener.

Tone Exercise: Tone Test

In this quick test of your own range of tone, call your voicemail and leave a message for yourself. Write a sentence or two to recite, so in each case you say the same words, but deliver them in different tones. Leave this message for each of the following scenarios:

- Happy to hear from the person
- Unhappy to hear from the person
- Sad
- Angry
- Talking to your boss
- Talking to your peer
- Talking to your subordinate
- Talking to a competitor
- Saying it like an actor you like
- Saying it like a recognizable politician
- Talking to a six-year-old

Play back your messages and see how you sound to yourself.

Tone Exercise: Tonal Variety

Choose a word like *okay* and deliberately say it out loud in a variety of ways—loud, quiet, breathy, kind, angry, tired, exasperated, and any other way you can think of.

Notice how different the word sounds to you with varying emotions, and consider how it could sound to others, and not always in a good way.

From these exercises, you can see that within you, you possess a wide variety of tones that you can use on purpose, for a purpose. The key with executive presence is to use the tone you want for the intent you want, recognizing that otherwise, you'll be unwittingly saying something you don't mean to.

Tone Exercise: Playback Critique

Go into your sent mail folder in your email system, and pull out the 10 most recent emails you sent to colleagues within your company. Read them aloud into a voice recorder. As you play them back to yourself, make notes about how you felt as you listen. What was your tone? Did it vary depending on the person? Depending on the message? Did you say nice things? Were your requests framed as demands or favors? How did you sign off?

Make a list of five things you did well in your messages and five things you'd like to change or avoid in the future.

Storytelling

My friend and his family were flying to Barbados. They were seated in first class, and my friend could hear a conversation in the coach bulkhead right behind their seats about a family whose members were separated between the two areas of the plane. The children were crying, and the parents had their hands full in the stressful situation, disturbing others around them.

My friend quietly gave up his family's seats in first class to allow the other family to be together. Obviously, the separated family was very appreciative.

At the luggage area, the two men talked, and the man originally in coach learned that the family who gave up their seats was staying at the resort he managed. In appreciation for the seat-switching gesture, the man arranged for his new friends to enjoy a week's vacation at the resort at no cost.

Reading the story, you aren't being told what to think, but you likely get the message that good things come from good actions. Storytelling is one of the oldest ways to deliver a message; after all, cavemen drew stories on stone walls; the Bible and the teachings of Buddha are all stories.

By using storytelling to communicate, you:

- Communicate in a more interesting fashion by drawing people in with the picture you paint. Stories are always more captivating than facts, claims, or platitudes.
- Resonate with your audience, making the experience more memorable and entertaining.
- Help others relate to you or the situation you wish to convey.
- Communicate values and beliefs without pontificating.
- Make people think and feel in a way that numbers and data presentation can't.
- Improve cross-cultural understanding of a situation.
- Build connectedness, credibility, and trust.
- Influence and motivate others with your experiences, causing them to think about their own.

Stories can relate what happened, convey an analogy, illustrate a point, or serve as an example. A good format to use when telling a story so you don't get carried away and go on and on is:

1. State the situation.

2. Explain what you did.

3. Tell the result.

You can draw out stories from others by asking them:

- Why they did it (whatever the situation).
- How they did it.

Remember the exercise in chapter 3 in which you wrote your autobiography? That material can be turned into stories to better explain your abilities, strengths, interests, or goals in a job interview, teach a lesson to your children, or help people connect with you.

To best use stories in those situations:

1. State your position or point of view.

2. Tell a story to illustrate (refrain from giving yourself the starring role or giving too much detailed minutiae).

3. Repeat your position that the story supports.

4. Invite questions or reactions from your listeners.

A good use of stories for cultivating executive presence is to pay attention to the successes of others and then relate those successes as stories. Instead of saying, "Juan did a great job on his presentation," you could illustrate with a story: "Juan was given the task of explaining our new technology—something even our technology consultants really hadn't been able to accomplish. He used an analogy of chopping wood, which none of us had actually done, but we, of course, all imagined we could do it. At the end of his presentation, he literally chopped some wood on stage in front of us. We laughed but definitely related to the simplicity of the technology instead of being overwhelmed by the vastness of it."

Storytelling Exercise: Your Story

1. Select an experience in your life that is important to you—perhaps an accomplishment or success.

2. Write the facts of what happened.

3. Enhance the facts with every point you can illustrate using the five senses.
4. Keep it truthful, but make it come alive. Make it engaging and relatable.
5. If you can add some surprise, such as a conflict you overcame (maybe there is a good guy and a bad guy in the scenario), include that element.
6. Omit irrelevant details.
7. Now select another memorable experience and complete steps 1 through 6 again.

Over time, you'll want to build up a repertoire of stories to use for every occasion (24 at minimum).

Story Development Exercise: Team-Building Analogy

1. Think of a point you need to make to motivate or influence your team (e.g., "Our sales team's goal for this year is to exceed last year's sales by 25 percent").
2. Think of an analogy for the position you are taking (e.g., it's a big mountain to climb). Is it an effective story? How will it be received?

Here's an example of a story-analogy:

We need to see what gear is needed for the mountain's climate and terrain.

Do we have the resources now, or do we need to acquire some?

We need to view the best way up the mountain. What possible routes are there?

What steps do we need to take to meet our sales goal? What sales techniques or incentives will help?

Instead of standing at the bottom of the mountain looking up, let's use creative thinking and imagine we are already at the top. Looking down from the top, we can see the various routes up. Let's talk about them.

Let's imagine we met our goal. Looking from the winning position, what enabled us to get there?

By using a relevant and illustrative analogy, you help explain a complex situation, which enables people to more readily grasp your vision.

Empathetic Storytelling Exercise: Acknowledge Different Perspectives

Think of a situation, such as a problem that needs to be solved. Then think about it from the perspective of all the people involved.

Example: A gorilla has escaped from the zoo.

- The zookeeper's perspective: I'm worried; my job is on the line for letting this happen.
- The gorilla's perspective: This is fun, with freedom like never before, but I'm getting a little hungry, because the zookeeper isn't here to feed me.

- The neighbors' perspective: We are worried about the safety of our kids, pets, and neighbors.
- The kids' perspective: This is so cool! Maybe we can get slingshots and go gorilla hunting. Or maybe we can put out food to attract it.
- The media's perspective: This is an exciting story and a nice break from 24/7 political coverage. I hope we encounter it first and scoop the other networks.

By considering your analogy from the perspective of all those involved, your story is more empathetic and wide-reaching among the audience you are trying to motivate and influence.

Verbal vs. Written Communication

Some leaders have great verbal presence but lack the same abilities in their written communication. For others, the opposite holds true. Because good leaders need both, we'll explore how they differ and consider the tenets of each communication style. By raising your awareness of their nuances and how they affect your messages, you can learn to communicate more effectively.

Verbal communication relies on tone of voice and body language to express meaning. Speed of speaking, volume, language, accent, eye contact, distance during interaction, and timing are all part of the effectiveness of a message. Nonverbal communication is all of the above, but without the words.

A problem with verbal communication is that it's in real time. The words and gestures that come from you have been delivered and cannot be edited. There's no backpedaling to undo words that didn't come out exactly as intended or that were expressed in a reactionary way. We'll talk about how advance planning can help avoid this dilemma.

Written communication is more effective to convey complex information, as it can be read and reread for understanding, documentation, and reporting, or to propose or persuade, and so on. You can spend as much time as needed to ensure the clarity, word choice, grammar, and punctuation of your message. But in written communication, you don't have all the nonverbal cues that you might depend on to communicate in person. That's why, for example, sarcasm doesn't translate well onto the page.

One problem with written communication is that even a small mistake in the rules of language can cause the reader to question or dismiss the authority of the person writing. Additionally, a reader who scans your writing might take something out of context and hold it against you. And, of course, words put into writing are documented, so always make sure they are defensible—that you stand behind them.

Remember, whether you're using written, verbal, or nonverbal communication, you are always communicating something. It's impossible to control how everyone will take everything that you say and do, but there are steps you can take to control the message you send.

When writing:

1. To start, write. Just go for it and get it all out. Make sure you write what others need to know, not just what you want them to know.

2. Set your writing aside for a day if possible, or even an hour.

3. Revisit what you wrote from the perspective of the reader.

4. Decide if what you wrote answers their questions and addresses their issues.

5. When you're pretty certain the content is there, try to cut words where you can. Edit as much as possible, then set it aside. Later, edit it again. Check each sentence and ask yourself, "Is this necessary? Is there a simpler way to say this?"

6. Use a thesaurus to expand your vocabulary, and avoid using the same word repeatedly. (Keep in mind that synonyms listed in a thesaurus don't always provide an exact match for the context you may be seeking. Double-check the meanings of new words in a dictionary.)

7. Look at your tone. Is this the tone you want to project? Adjust as necessary.

8. Now, reread the message and find the strongest sentence. See if you can make that sentence your first. You want the premise of your message to be clear in the first sentence or two, and not further than the third.

9. Make sure each sentence makes them want to read the next one.

10. Finally, read your message with the goal of looking for something new and interesting to say; put your own personal spin on it.

In academia, complicated, precise, and verbose writing is valued. In business, simplicity and directness are valued. In both, a leader is judged.

Today, verbal communication goes further than a one-to-one in-person chat or phone call. It also includes meetings, video calls, online trainings, and presentations.

With verbal communication, you can follow all the steps for written communication. If you do that, it will separate you from the others and enhance your executive presence. However, there are a few differences in how you can approach verbal communication, which we'll explore. The most important step, though, is preparation.

One CEO told me, "Every time I say something out loud, I say it to myself first to see how it sounds and then change it as necessary." I asked, "Doesn't that take a long time?" He said, "In the beginning it did, but now I'm pretty practiced."

In-person, one-on-one, this is where executive presence shines. There are conflicting studies and reports on the dwindling attention span of modern people, but regardless of your beliefs on this issue, it pays to take steps to make sure you are succinct, clear, and empathetic.

When communicating verbally:

1. Think about what you want to say. Clear thinking results in clear speaking. Ask yourself: *What am I trying to say?*

2. Write notes about what you want to say. The act of writing helps you remember. The listener wants to know "what's in this discussion for me?" If you're new to this or tend to stumble over your words, it can be helpful to write out your entire statement. You don't need to write every word if you're a natural speaker—in this case, bullet points will usually suffice.

3. Take responsibility for the interchange. Instead of asking, "Did you understand what I'm trying to get across?" which puts the onus on them, ask, "Was my explanation put in a clear manner?"

4. Use a thesaurus when writing notes to avoid using the same word many times. Just like in writing, make sure the word you choose retains the same meaning as the one you're replacing—the thesaurus doesn't always provide an exact match.

5. Strive to be original or interesting by using a story, example, or little-known detail or fact to explain your point.

6. When you've said what needs to be said, stop.

7. Leave them with a smile.

Written Communication Exercise: State Your Case with Purpose

1. Think of an issue that is important to you. Determine the outcome you want to achieve with a 100-word written case for some action to be taken.
2. Decide what you need to write to achieve the goal. Incorporate storytelling, empathy, emotional intelligence, and intellectual intelligence.
3. Write with clarity, simplicity, and completeness of thought.
4. Check for grammar, punctuation, tense, tone, and word choice.
5. Now, rewrite the content from a contrasting point of view. Argue with yourself and debate in a way that flexes your writing skills.
6. Rewrite your original case with what you learned from the opposite position.

By forcing yourself to take the opposite perspective, you see things from another point of view, but you also see where your own position requires strengthening.

Try the same process with a simple email, and you'll see an improved message.

Writing Exercise: Diversify Your Message

1. Pull out an old document that you've written.
2. Go through it and look for repeated use of the same word. For example, if you were proposing a new project, note the number of times you used the word *new*.
3. Think for a few minutes—go to the thesaurus if needed—and see where you can replace the word while retaining your message. Would another word add interest and impact, such as *leading-edge*, *progressive*, *novel*, *latest*, or *advanced*?

Verbal Communication Exercise: Build a Clear Message

In this exercise, you'll record some conversations with people who won't mind (and have agreed to be part of this exercise). Explain that you aren't analyzing them but yourself.

1. Make your presentation (such as a pitch or perspective on a subject) to the other person. Invite them to ask questions or comment on the subject.
2. Later, listen to the recording. As you listen, try to put yourself in the other person's shoes to identify areas where you were clear and where you weren't.
3. If you discover any sentences that were unclear, rewrite them in your head and say them to yourself. Mentally rewrite them until you have the best version memorized.

You can do a version of this exercise several times a day. Every time you leave a voicemail message, choose the option to listen to your message and rerecord if necessary. Spending a few minutes doing that every day will measurably improve your clarity and confidence. Most importantly, you are working to ensure the message you send is the one you intend.

What's Professional?

In carpentry they say, "Measure twice, cut once." In today's working world, it is wise to think twice and speak once. Of course, there is a balance. You don't have to talk only about work with your colleagues. It's good to connect with them on a deeper level as you get to know them. But your goal in doing so is to make others comfortable and show empathy, so naturally you'll want to avoid anything that will make them uncomfortable. Remember that all people are not necessarily like you—everyone has a different comfort zone. Therefore, steer away from topics like:

- **Religion.** It's acceptable to let people know your faith and what it means to you, but not to assume anything about someone else's faith. Refrain from using humor or negativity in reference to others' religious beliefs, and definitely don't try to convert them.
- **Politics.** While you might feel strongly about your party or candidate, it is poor workplace etiquette to put down others' political preferences or try to persuade them to your side. It won't work. It's likely futile. It might even be construed as using your power to force someone to think like you. Think about it: Does their opinion change yours in the slightest?
- **Your or their sex life.** This subject has no place in the workplace. Not only does it make people uncomfortable, but it also can place

you on precarious legal thin ice. Sexual harassment claims can come from words, looks, or touch, and they can kill a career.

- **Problems with family members and friends.** Unless you are seeking help from your company's employee assistance program, discussing what's going on with parents, children, spouses, or friends is not going to build executive presence. Doing so lends itself to gossip, and it can cause people to question your ability to control your own life.

- **How much you are paid.** Talking about green is a rather "green" move—it's a flub often made by amateurs who are trying to build themselves up by using their salary to attempt to impress others. This is immature, and it's a sensitive topic. However, sometimes the taboo against talking about your salaries at work can get in the way of rectifying inequalities like the gender pay gap—if a woman is being paid less than a man in the same role with similar seniority and performance, she should be aware of that. But that is a sensitive conversation, not to be had lightly. It's taboo for a reason. Generally, income and career ambitions are subjects best left between you and your immediate supervisor, and HR if necessary.

- **Your health.** If people learn about a sickness—mental or physical—they are likely to look for it. Even when you have no problems, they'll remember that you did, and it will shed doubt on your energy, ability, and advancement potential. There are things you'll need to share to explain an absence, and certainly if you suffer from anything contagious that may affect others, your immediate supervisor and human resources should be informed.

Outside of these select areas, there are countless other topics you can use to get to know, connect with, and bond with people.

Building and Improving Relationships

A big reason for building relationships at work is personal job satisfaction. When you work with others you like being with, you will enjoy work more and want to get up and go there every day. Building relationships also increases your chances of advancing in your career and being recognized for your achievements. You'll feel like part of a team and less intimidated by any one coworker who might be toxic.

It's the same thing you do in your personal life: You notice someone, start a conversation, and make a connection. You are friendly and initiate an exchange where you ask people questions and tell people about yourself. Something like, "I noticed you're really good at _____. I've been trying to get into that area, but my stumbling block is _____. Any suggestions? By the way, my name is _____."

Initiating interactions is the key. Don't wait until others approach you; it's very likely that they are more nervous than you. When you go places, walk in with an open mind and without judgment. Pay attention and look for an opportunity to talk to people. Explore without fear of rejection, and resist the urge to hang out in the bathroom or look at your phone—the road to executive presence requires courage. Just bust in there and start connecting, even if it simply means looking for another person standing alone.

Most people are as uncomfortable as you are talking to someone new, but most want to get to know others, so if you're the one who breaks the ice, you will be extra welcome and remembered. Consider the fact you have hundreds of opportunities in a single day to initiate an exchange that could develop into a lasting positive relationship. And if not, it's fine. Most interactions are simply about being nice to each other in the moment. If your effort with one person turns sour, consider it practice and try again.

With executive presence, you learn how to make yourself an asset in any situation. Even when you aren't in charge, people will see you as in charge because you take the initiative.

Building Relationships Exercise: Executive Emulation

Look for five or six people you admire in your company, your community, or even the public eye. Whenever you have a chance, watch them speak. Observe how they present information. Pay attention to what they say and how they say it: their tone, body language, and choice of words.

Notice what fits your personality and what you can do similarly. Try it in a future conversation or presentation. How does it feel? Now take this a step further: Note what they do that would stretch your comfort zone, and then try that in your next conversation or presentation.

Building and Improving Relationships Exercise: Breaking Barriers

Make a list of things in this book that seem too difficult or anxiety-provoking for you. You can look beyond this book, too—simply consider, what are you scared to do? Every day or week, try to conquer one item on the list. Don't give up until you've tried each item on the list at least 10 times.

Building and Improving Relationships Exercise: Networking Challenge

1. Find a buddy and go to a networking or social event together. Agree in advance to try to meet and learn something about as many people as you can. Separate once there and go about observing, and, where possible, initiate some engagement. If you're new to networking or not comfortable with the prospect, agree to stick together for a few minutes so you can learn the ropes. Observe, and then set out to make your own connections.

2. Keep track of the names of people you met and the information you learned. Make a mental note of something significant you learned from each connection.

3. Take a break after a half hour, meet up with your buddy, and compare notes on your successes. Discuss what you learned, such as what conversation starters were the most effective. Then go out for round two.

4. At the end of the event, compare your experiences. Who spoke to more people? Who had more fruitful conversations? Did either of you make meaningful connections worth following up on?

5. In the next day or two, follow up with connections you made, thanking them for their time and showing interest in the conversation you had by revisiting any relevant points (e.g., "I really enjoyed hearing your thoughts on our new roofing products. If you want to talk more about it, maybe we can share your thoughts with R&D").

Managing Conflict/Difficult Conversations

I like to help people visualize executive presence as the ability to "seamlessly fit in and effortlessly stand out." The "stand out" part can be tricky, because some people will be jealous of your success. I've surveyed many CEOs over the years and asked, "What was the biggest surprise about making it to the top?" A frequent answer: "How many enemies I got."

It's human nature to envy others' achievements and even to try to feel better about oneself by knocking someone else down. Sometimes called office politics, it's disconcerting, especially when you are working diligently to be a genuine individual and cultivate executive presence through empathy and generosity.

One of the main reasons executives are sent to me for coaching is to manage that very issue. Conflict is inevitable, regardless of how infallible your behavior may be. It's natural, and it happens in every relationship. Because some dissent is unavoidable, you'll want to learn to manage it.

There will always be some conflict. It might go underground, but it can resurface at a most inopportune time. Conflict avoidance is the number one problem with employees, according to many CEOs.

A productive perspective about such a disagreement is that it's an opportunity for change, growth, new understanding, and improved communication. Consistency in style of leadership and communication can help with managing conflict and navigating difficult conversations, along with the common objective to resolve that issue and make sure it doesn't resurface. (Another issue will always surface.)

To start addressing the issue, make the decision to have a constructive (not destructive) conversation. Clarify the source of the conflict: What is the real problem? Ask questions of all sides to find out what needs are not being met. Do this in private and listen intently.

One CEO told me, "If you berate someone in front of people, you'll lose everything. Take them into your office. Explain the problem, how it occurred, and what needs to be done about it. Then encourage them to go and do it. That way, you create loyalty instead of resentment."

Here, you'll need to enlist discipline to listen instead of talking, even if it requires you to bite your tongue. Let all parties involved have their say. Set some ground rules: no name calling, no blame, no profanity.

After allowing people to talk it out, take it on yourself to quietly and confidentially investigate. Learn what happened from other perspectives. Remember the gorilla who escaped from the zoo (page 69)? Everyone had different perspectives.

Ask the people involved to brainstorm a solution that would be satisfactory to all. Insist that everyone makes some compromise. Together, choose the best resolution and think about how to implement it; make it the responsibility of everyone involved. Consider preemptive measures to avoid the conflict in the future. Agree on them.

Check in on how things are going in a week, then in a month, and be ready to step in with preemptive measures. The idea is to address it quickly, get it out of everyone's system, and then get over it.

We all experience friction in our families, our neighborhoods, our communities, and our companies. As a leader, you have varying control of the outcome depending on the number of people and dissimilarity of viewpoints. But if you remain consistent in how you approach conflict, you are the leader. And you are exhibiting executive presence.

Preemptive Conflict Exercise: Be Prepared

No matter how much you try to avoid conflict or problems, they will occur. Think about a project you are working on right now or a team you are working with. Try to project down the line: What could cause a problem in the future? For example, what consequence would a missed deadline have? What would happen if funding ends? What if bullying or dissent occurs among team members? Or if someone produces poor-quality output? Any of those can happen on a daily basis.

1. Consider the risks. Before a problem arises, think about what could happen.
2. Consider options to deal with it. What might you say or do, how, and to whom?
3. Assess the viability of the options. In addition to communicating, what actions can you take? What behaviors can you adopt?
4. Weigh others' likely responses. Consider how various people involved may react.

Just preparing for a potential conflict takes some of the apprehension away and sets you up to react thoughtfully. Additionally, preparing for it may shed light on preemptive action steps so the conflict doesn't occur.

Repeat this exercise on a regular basis. Consider making this part of your personal Monday-morning meeting as you look at your week ahead.

Managing Conflict Exercise: Candor Before Conflict

To teach one another how to avoid conflict, it can actually help to engage in a form of candid conflict. Using this exercise can fix a problem situation before it happens.

1. Select an individual that you are generally on good terms with. Tell them that you are doing a two-way exercise so you can learn how to work together even more effectively. Explain that you selected them because you already have a positive working relationship with them.

2. Ask, "What can I do to make you feel heard and respected? If you tell me candidly, it will make it easier for me to do what will make you feel that respect and attention." Write down what the person says. Then respond in kind by explaining, "I feel heard and respected when you _____ (e.g., send me updates on your projects)." Then say, "How can I make it easier for you to do that?" Write down what you learn.

3. Thank them for their candor. If necessary, apologize for any past oversights discovered during this conversation, and then fix the situation based on what you learned.

Next, take this same exercise to someone who is less congenial but nonetheless, you must work together. This kind of candid discussion can boost your chances of changing the dynamic between you.

This exercise can also be adapted to use with a manager. For example, "What can I do to make your job easier? Your feedback will help me better understand your needs and wants." Then you can respond, "I feel appreciated and valued when you do _____," followed by, "How can I make it easier for you to do that?"

Regardless of the person you conduct this exercise with, the result is the same: The more you set mutual expectations, the more understanding there will be, and the fewer misinterpretations will occur.

Managing Conflict Exercise: Who Would Win?

Get four people together—two to participate in the exercise and two judges.

Have the two participants stand face-to-face. Have one of the judges count to three, and on three, each participant will shout out the name of an animal. The two animals are going to fight. The first person gets two minutes to explain why their animal would win the fight. The second person gets two minutes to respond and counter the first attack by explaining why their animal would win.

Each of the judges gets to ask one question of each participant. Then the judges confer with each other and choose a winner. If the two judges disagree, the game is repeated.

Now debrief. How did the exercise feel to each participant? To the judges? What were the attitudes of the participants? The body language? Ask the participants, "Were you able to listen to each other and respond directly to each other's imaginary attacks, or were you each just telling different stories past each other?"

Takeaways

- Communication is key to executive presence; it shows you to be a professional, allows you to capture an audience, and helps you build relationships, manage conflict, and navigate difficult conversations.
- To be more effective, you can communicate with people to find out how they need or want to be communicated with.
- Sometimes the best communication is to simply listen. This is how we learn from others.

- Aim for a boardroom tone: loud enough to be heard, at a relaxed pace, and accompanied by consistent body language.
- Stories that others can identify with or relate to build interest and understanding.
- Be as professional in your online words as you are in person. Don't let the comfort of working from home result in communication complacency.
- Conflict is a common issue among CEOs; however, it's also an opportunity for change, growth, new understanding, and improved communication.

CHAPTER FIVE

Comportment

"She hurried, but she did not rush."
"He makes an entrance, even when exiting."

We've covered a lot of soft skills that are essential to executive presence, including communication, leadership, self-awareness, empathy, and emotional intelligence. But no one can tell if you've got those skills just by looking at you. You can't go around wearing a sign on your lapel stating, "I expect acceptance and I give acceptance. My leadership style is democratic and my favorite way to communicate is through storytelling."

However, long before you open your mouth, people size you up. I venture to say we all do it, to a degree. I can tell if someone has executive presence from a football field away, by their posture, walk, and pace. If they move with precision and purpose, they will probably lead that way.

With executive presence, you show others what you want them to see. You don't leave it to chance. You take full responsibility for the effect you have on others.

Business Etiquette

Part of the code of executive presence is business etiquette. It's the expectation of social behavior and how people interact in a workplace. It varies from one organization to another, but it always has the same purpose: to respect and protect people, time, and resources.

If you have etiquette, you can handle nearly any situation, whether you are working in a new company or working with people in a different company or even in a different country. Work etiquette transcends industries, countries, and cultures. Of course, as it crosses these spaces, it will pick up certain idiosyncratic behaviors and expectations, but we are all part of humanity. Human nature connects us, regardless of the language we speak.

Business etiquette—this professionalism—is about your relationship with other people, not about following some specific list of rules and regulations. Etiquette sets a mutually respectful atmosphere, ensures civilized communication, makes others comfortable and secure, enhances your personal brand, and ultimately makes for a more productive workplace.

Without such guidelines, it's simply more difficult to work together. Poor examples are set, people are demoralized, and everyone is held back.

Here are five universal guidelines for business etiquette:

1. Pay attention to **names**.

2. Pay attention to **manners**.

3. Pay attention to **courtesy**.

4. Pay attention to **discretion**.

5. Show through your words and actions that you are paying attention to these things.

Names

When you call somebody by their name, you make that person feel recognized as an individual who is valued and important to you. They remember that you remembered and will more readily be willing to work and engage with you. It's a simple gesture that you can do to uphold the self-esteem of others, show you pay attention, and set yourself apart from the many others who forget names.

Pronunciation is also important. People know how to pronounce their own name, so if you get it wrong, they know you're getting it wrong. So even if you think it should be pronounced a different way, make sure you do it their way. It's fine, even respectful, to ask someone two or three times how to pronounce their name if necessary.

When you meet someone, listen carefully when they introduce themself and say their name. Repeat the name right then, and if it is unusual, ask if you are pronouncing it correctly. Then be sure to use it in that conversation, both for the reasons previously outlined and for your own memorization.

To help people remember your name when you begin a conversation, start with "Debra here! I'd like to check in on_____." Don't feel uncomfortable saying your own name. They may have forgotten it. Make it easy for them to look good by reminding them of your name.

It's also important to respect people's gender pronouns. You won't always know gender identity by looking at someone or hearing their voice, so if a situation arises where you need to know, you can ask. If you ignore or assume, they may feel disrespected, invalidated, and alienated. If you do not know whether the person prefers him/his, her/hers, them/theirs, or ze/hir (ze replaces she/he/they, and hir, pronounced "here," replaces her/hers/him/his/they/theirs), it's safe to simply use their name instead of the pronoun.

Here are examples of accepted pronoun usage:

- Chris drank her drink because she was thirsty.
- Chris drank his drink because he was thirsty.

- Chris drank their drink because they were thirsty.
- Chris drank hir drink because ze was thirsty.
- Chris drank Chris's drink because Chris was thirsty.

Manners

We all grew up with some degree of emphasis placed on manners. Treating people with courtesy and politeness makes any interpersonal exchange more enjoyable, both for you and for those you come in contact with. Here are some examples of good manners:

- Stand when being introduced to someone.
- Make eye contact, especially when shaking hands, speaking, or listening.
- Speak clearly so you're easily understood.
- Respond when spoken to, emailed, voicemailed, or texted.
- Don't apologize unless you have something to apologize for.

Why stand when you are being introduced? This gesture shows respect but also puts you on an equal standing with the individual. You do not want to have to look up at them, and they don't want to look down on you.

Making eye contact shows that you are in the moment, giving others the attention they deserve. The value of an introduction or handshake is lost (but not forgotten) if you are looking in another direction.

Speaking clearly and with purpose, in an audible manner and self-aware tone, helps ensure the words you are saying align with your comportment.

When someone speaks, it's helpful to show interest by nodding or leaning forward. When someone has a question, any answer is better than nothing—even a simple "no" will often suffice. Whether the question was asked over the phone or by text or email, it's poor form to leave people hanging. People can generally accept good news or bad news, but it's irritating when there is no news.

Unnecessarily saying you're sorry may seem like an odd thing to identify as a breach of manners. Of course, if you offend someone or do something wrong, you'll want to apologize quickly and sincerely, and make sure you don't do it again. But saying "sorry" all the time, like when you are walking down the hallway while another person is coming toward you, isn't necessarily polite because you're placing a burden on the other person to assure you that it's okay. Additionally, telling someone "I'm sorry for being late" when in fact you made no effort to be on time, didn't care about being late, and will do it again is not being sorry nor sincere. We all know someone like this, and they do not have executive presence.

Courtesy

Courtesy involves being aware of others in the room or on the call. Acts of courtesy might include:

- Acknowledging others as they arrive.
- Introducing those who might not know each other.
- Listening politely and showing interest.
- Not interrupting.
- Subtly pointing out when others are trying to speak.
- Asking questions.
- Engaging quieter members in the discussion.
- Thanking people for their participation.
- Gesturing for others to leave the room ahead of you.

Discretion

Whether you are a leader or hoping to be one, trust is a characteristic that will earn you loyalty. You build trust by showing discretion and respecting people's right to privacy. When you are entrusted with or learn private or sensitive information, as long as nothing unethical is being shared, you'll want to tuck that information away in a file deep in your mind.

Business Etiquette Exercise: Expand Your World

Make a point of engaging with every person you work with who has a different cultural background from your own. Be sure that you know for certain that their customs or culture is different—don't assume just because they look different from you that they practice other customs. Watch for signals that they practice other customs. Ask them:

- How do you prefer to be greeted or bid farewell?
- What language does your extended family speak? (Language is a better proxy for culture than place. "Where are you from?" can be considered offensive.)
- Do you have customs or norms for conduct that are different from what you experience in this workplace?

Make note of differences that you learn about, and make it a point to honor that information; even use it with that person at an appropriate time in the future. It will show that you pay attention. But don't overemphasize it, either. Talk more about commonalities than differences.

Business Etiquette Exercise: How to Remember Names

1. When you meet someone new, be alert for their name. You might be shaking hands or fist bumping and saying your name right after they say theirs. Be sure to focus on the name. Most of us don't even hear the other person's name because we are too busy saying ours.

2. Immediately repeat their name out loud, using it in the very next comment that you make to the person (e.g., "It's great to meet you, Jerry").

3. If possible and appropriate, use their name again within a few minutes ("Jerry, what department do you work in?").

4. At the first opportunity, discreetly write the name down somewhere.

5. Use their name when you are talking to someone about the event you attended ("I met Jerry from marketing. Didn't you work together on the annual report?").

To test your improvement after this exercise, reflect on how many times you used someone's name today. Try to increase this practice each day. There is very little chance you will overuse someone's name—or forget it.

Business Etiquette Exercise: Mind Your Manners

The next time you're at work, pay scrupulous attention to your manners. Even if you're typically an informal person, explain that you're practicing and make it fun. Ask your colleagues to participate, and ask them their favorite act of formality and politeness. Try to get a game going around the office.

On the Virtual Workplace

Working remotely removes a lot of face time from the equation. The benefits of remote work are at least partially offset by the lack of human interaction, as people learned during the COVID-19 epidemic. It became necessary to fight against loneliness, isolation, and even too much freedom.

However, the same discipline required to do work in an office is required to do virtual work—it's just that you may have to work a little harder in the virtual environment to demonstrate executive presence. But the opportunity is still there.

Two things to remember when executive presence is your goal:

1. Everything you do in person needs to be done even when not in person. This is because others can see your expression (and your shirt and hair) and hear your tone (and your dog and your child) on a phone or video call. Of course, tone can also be discerned from a text or email. We've explored how words translate differently depending on the tone we use.

2. If you don't consistently work as if you were there in person, you'll dull your skill set, diminishing your effectiveness when you return in person.

Some things to avoid during remote work:

- **Distractions.** Get agreement from the people in your home that you will have alone time or quiet time. Ignore the load of laundry that could be done and instead complete a task or project without taking yourself away from it. Wear noise-canceling headphones if necessary.

- **Overworking.** Compartmentalize your time. When the day is done, close the laptop, and put the phone down. Do your required hourly or project commitment, then stop. One report stated that people working remotely put in an average of three extra weeks over the course of a year.

- **Complacency.** Without having to shave and shower and dress up, it's easy to be too casual—about everything. What goes on in your body spills over to your head. To appear professional, never mind executive, you'll need to maintain self-discipline in your attitude, leadership, communication, manners, and appearance (which we'll explore). Pretend that your boss could walk into your workspace at any moment—you want to make sure they see and conclude what you want them to.
- **Negativity.** Instead of complaining, choose to adopt a positive perspective. Remind yourself of the benefits (e.g., no commute cost or time, comfortable dress, autonomy, time spent with family, freedom to take a break during the workday and go for a run).

You can still be productive even when work is quiet:
- Send an email to a business leader doing interesting work and compliment them.
- Volunteer to give a webinar to a nonprofit.
- Write a note of appreciation to a coworker.
- Contact someone who is angry with you and try to resolve the disagreement.
- Work on your skills in a desired area—like executive presence!
- Follow your interests.

Body Language

Your body language encompasses how you look, move, listen, and react. Eye contact, pace, space, voice, facial expressions, and gestures all play into body language. Coordination of these signals is key: You want what is going on inside your head to be consistently displayed in your physicality. People believe what they see, and they see what you show them.

If your attitude is one of competence, confidence, and comfort in your skin, great—show it so people will believe it.

Here are some tips to ensure the message you send through body language is the one you intend:

- **Get into your desired mindset.** Breathe deeply and think about your intended message and how you want to convey it. Reflect on the presence you will exude.
- **Use your entire physical being to express yourself.** Pay attention to the angle of your head (straight on, chin up), your facial expression (gentle smile), your shoulders (erect, not rounded), the fit of your clothes, and the position of your arms and hands (relaxed).
- **Move purposefully, even a little slowly:** whether you are adjusting your eyeglasses, moving through the room, or turning a page. Rapid movements make you appear nervous.
- **Have a game plan for how you'll approach the room.** Pause before walking into a meeting, breathing to relax. With good posture, walk into the room. Pause again to determine where you want to move to, and sit. Nonverbally announce yourself with your movements and pause. With good posture, approach anyone you plan to meet and greet them.
- **During this time, develop your presence by subtraction.** Stop yourself from any nervous or distracting behavior, such as twisting your hair around your finger, touching your nose or your mouth, tapping your foot, or fiddling with your wedding ring. If you do have to stim, you can carry a small fidget spinner, a rubber band, or even a pebble.
- **Do something different.** To stand out, you can first observe how most are acting. Then, without being odd, subtly do something a bit differently. The smallest change can make a big difference.
- **Be open-minded.** Don't try to read other people's body language, even though you can expect them to read yours.

Instead, pay attention and be thoughtful, and solicit their opinions whether or not you sense they might disagree with you.

Here are some key elements of strong body language:

- **Eye contact.** This is a good thing, but there's a bit of art involved. Sometimes eye contact can feel invasive. You want others to know you're attentive, but you don't want them to feel like you are boring into their soul. One way to give eye contact but not feel so invasive when you are standing at a distance is to look at the person's nose or mouth. They will still feel like you are talking to them directly. Avoid this practice if you are standing close; instead, you can alternate good eye contact with gestures or glances in the air as if you are thinking, to the door if you're referring to other departments, etc.

- **Pace.** Slow down your speech reasonably to a point where you sound cool, calm, and relaxed. In this fast-paced world, someone who is comfortable in their skin is enjoyable to listen to and easier to engage with than someone who appears harried and frenetic.

- **Space.** It's important not to invade someone's personal space by getting too close, but if you don't get close enough, you can't be heard, you can't hear, and you look timid. If someone gets closer to you than you are comfortable with, turn your body away from them a bit rather than stepping back, if possible. The whole room will open up, and your actions won't appear evasive. Be more assertive if that doesn't work.

- **Facial expression.** Of all the body language that you use, this is most important. Your face is what people see, even behind a face mask. Use your "ready" face as your baseline. In sports, there's usually a ready position—how you hold your racket, your baseball bat, or your golf club. With your facial ready position, pretend you're getting ready for the other person to throw you a ball. Look aware and interested. As one person put it, "It's the expression I have when I'm sitting on the deck looking at boats and birds." The key to executive presence is to learn how to keep it when you are angry, glad, concerned, hurried, stressed, and so on. Your reaction to various triggers is contagious—by leading calmly, others are reassured that things are under control.

Body Language Exercise: Eye Contact, Nose Contact?

Try this exercise with some friends. Explain to them what you will be doing. Try giving them a little more eye contact than you're used to, or even a lot more. Try talking to them but look at their nose or mouth. Ask them afterward if you were giving them good eye contact and if it made them comfortable. Then reverse roles and ask them to do the same to you. See how it feels and provide feedback to them.

Body Language Exercise: Speak Up

Interesting fact: Most people speak at a lower volume than they should. To test this, gather a few friends to play a game. Invite one person to talk about something enjoyable: a family vacation, a new restaurant, a pet. As the person talks, have the others encourage the speaker to speak louder and bigger, using gestures. Encourage the speaker to go as big as they can.

Ask the speaker how they think they sounded. They will probably say that they felt like they were shouting, but likely they were speaking at the volume they should be, particularly for a presentation.

Body Language Exercise: Nonverbal Communication

Following are five sentences/ideas. Your task is to communicate them without using any words (including sign language), but rather with gestures and body language. Practice this in front of a mirror, or ask someone to watch you and give you feedback:

1. "I have an idea that would solve that problem!"
2. "I hear your point and respect your opinion, but I disagree."
3. "You are a great role model for me."
4. "I like your outfit today!"
5. "I hear that you are concerned, but I have this situation under control."

How did it feel to use body language to convey these points, and what did you learn about nonverbal communication? If someone watched your performance, ask them for feedback and then challenge them to give it a try.

Posture

Posture is an obvious and telling part of body language. Most of the time, when your parents told you to "straighten up," they were talking about your posture.

When you straighten up, you appear taller. That in itself is powerful: Studies have shown that taller people make more money. You also improve your speaking apparatus (diaphragm and vocal cords), you take a couple inches off your waist, and you project confidence and look like a winner.

Think of the losing football team on the sideline—players hunched over, heads hanging down. The winning players on the opposite sideline look like giants with their proud, bobbing, upright bearing. I've seen a CEO compliment one of his people and watched as the person seemed to grow two inches in front of everyone's eyes just by standing up straighter.

Social psychologist Brené Brown explains that practicing "power posing" can help make people take you seriously and respect you. You can practice this by placing your hands on your hips, pushing your chest out, and holding your chin up.

One way to remember to maintain good posture is to wear tailored clothes to reinforce your bearing. For instance, suit jackets tend to keep you upright, because the garment is built for that position. Wearing loose and flowy clothes sends a signal to your body to relax and hunch over.

Posture Exercise: Wall Work

Stand with your back against a wall. Pull your heels in so they are up against the wall. Notice how this position is stretching your chest muscles. Put the back of your head against the wall, too.

Stand there and breathe a few times. Then, holding that posture, walk away from the wall. That, my friend, is the ideal posture position for your body.

Do this exercise several times a day. Like with any habit, your muscles will eventually default into the desired position without the wall.

Posture Exercise 2: Build Good Habits

Return to the wall in the previous exercise and do the adjustment, then walk away from the wall. As you walk away, roll your shoulders up and back. This will relax the shoulders so you don't look so stiff.

If you are sitting and reading this, right now, suck in your stomach, lift your rib cage, roll your shoulders up and back down, and keep the posture.

If you have to correct your posture 100 times today, that is okay. With self-control, it might require only 98 times tomorrow and 95 the next day. That's how you retrain your body.

Posture Exercise 3: Sit Up Straight

Standing and walking with good posture are important, but so is sitting with good posture. Let's face it: It's comfortable to slouch, and when working at home, we don't always have the perfect setup, especially if we're working on the couch or at the kitchen table.

To improve your sitting posture, sit all the way back in your chair. Place a small rolled-up towel or cushion behind your mid-back to protect your spine's natural curve. Bend your knees at a right angle and keep them the same height, or a bit higher, than your hips. Place your feet flat on the floor. You may need to find a different chair or place a footrest at your feet.

There are back supports you can purchase online to give you good sitting posture, but they need to be adjusted once you stand up, so every time you sit or stand you have to readjust. Not worth it. Better to simply be aware and develop a good sitting practice without a gadget.

Takeaways

- People look at you and decide your leadership capability in a matter of seconds based on the way you walk, talk, and move. It's not fair, and it's often not accurate, but it's human nature. You cannot totally control what they conclude, but you can steer them in a positive direction with your comportment.
- Resist the urge to quickly judge anyone when you meet them. Give people the benefit of the doubt; accept their character, motive, and behavior; and reserve judgment until they have proven themselves.
- As a leader, your etiquette makes for a comfortable, respectful, civilized working atmosphere, enhances your brand, and results in a more productive workplace.
- Remembering names makes others feel valued and sets you apart from the many who forget names.
- Executive presence involves keeping the same demeanor when you are angry, glad, concerned, hurried, stressed, etc.

CHAPTER SIX

Appearances

Life isn't fair. People judge you on your looks. But in all fairness, don't you judge others on their looks, too? It's our nature to observe and conclude. It protects us. It excites us. It even entertains us. We love to check out people and form an opinion. And it's generally okay as long as we do it without prejudice, or at least honestly acknowledge the prejudice to ourselves if it's there.

The goal here is not to make you look like a businessperson or an executive. The goal is for you to look like you—just the best version of you. And although we want to be ourselves, there are many excellent examples we can look to in order to understand the power of appearances. I think of author and professor Dr. Cornel West—to me, he is unmistakable but also uncompromising in his appearance, and he always looks good. Whom do you think of?

Image

Image is a multifaceted concept. There is your self-image, which is the mental picture you have of yourself—maybe it's that you are an attractive, smart, happy, intelligent person. Then there is the image that is the perception people have of you based on your appearance. Ideally, those two images aren't far apart. (There is a third image, and that's the one people see when they really get to know you, but for now, we'll focus on first impressions.)

On the flip side, maybe you suffer from a negative self-image. If you view yourself as unattractive, unintelligent, unhappy, or not worthy of attention, you will project that about yourself, and people will certainly pick up on it. People believe what you show them. They figure you know yourself better than anyone, so they take you as you present yourself. One Texas university professor told me that if a new student appears to be smart, enthusiastic, and dedicated, but isn't really, it takes six months to find out. On the other hand, if a person seems quiet and dull but is in fact smart, enthusiastic, and dedicated, it takes six months to find that out, too.

Sure, image is superficial. Of course, it's really what's inside that counts (that third image we discover when we really get to know somebody). And actions speak loudest of all, over time. But superficial appearances play a role in our lives, and it doesn't do you any favors to ignore your own. Rather than say to yourself, "I just want to be me, and I don't care what people think about me," say to yourself, "I just want to be me, and I want other people to see me being myself."

You don't need to worry and fret over what people think, though. That's their responsibility; you can't do much about it, so leave it be. Your goal is to consistently and deliberately conduct yourself in a way that makes you appear memorable, impressive, credible, genuine, trusted, liked, cool, calm, collected, confident, and competent—because you are! Your image is never a façade if you believe in the way you carry yourself.

Your personal brand sums up your unique promise of value. It's not your job title, but it is something that others will use to try to classify you. So, think about how you introduce your job to people. Instead of just saying, "I'm a hairdresser," you could add, "I make other people look good." Instead of just saying, "I'm in _____ sales," you could say, "People look to me for the latest information on _____ before they buy, and I help connect them with the most highly rated products."

If you were to ask me what I do, I wouldn't say, "I'm an executive coach." I'd say, "I coach people to be more memorable, impressive, credible, genuine, trusted, liked, confident, and competent."

As for you, be yourself, but remember, your self can change. As a thinking adult, you can be a combination of the best of whatever you were raised with plus whatever you've been exposed to. It's never just about where you started but where you choose to go and end up as. You never stop growing—take all that growth with you and let it shape you.

I met a CEO at an airport concourse, and even from a distance, I could see this man standing with good posture, holding his trench coat draped over one arm. He was neatly attired from head to shoes. I commented, "When I saw you from a distance, I thought you looked very distinguished." He smiled and good-naturedly replied, "With the money they pay me, I have to look like this."

Another time, I was talking to a lawyer at a ski resort in Colorado. Every attendee had ski sweaters, down jackets, knit hats, and ski boots. But the New York lawyer wore a suit and tie. I kidded him, "You're pretty fancy here in these mountains." He responded, "I choose to look the part wherever I am." Talk about knowing who you are.

Image Exercise: Build Your Personal Brand

To explore your own personal brand, review the story exercise from chapter 3 (page 37) to remind yourself who you are and what you've done. Consider what you want to be known for going forward.

Write a brand statement of one or two sentences explaining these three things:

1. What you are best at
2. Whom it benefits
3. How you do it distinctively

Image Exercise: Just Watch

The next time you are in a public place where lots of people are passing by, put your phone away and just watch. Notice yourself forming judgments about passersby. Notice what they are wearing, how they are walking, their mood, speed, and comportment. Let yourself speculate about them. Of course, you will never know if your conclusion about the person is accurate, but the exercise is to make you aware of how judgments are formed and what people may be concluding about you.

Image Exercise: The Campaign

1. Imagine you are running for office, but it's a pure personality contest without any policy at stake. Write down how you would try to appeal personally to voters—not on policy but on personality. Would you be "the person you want to have a beer with" or "the woman with the creative ideas" or "the family man"? Go into as much specificity as you can, outlining how you would want your voters to see you—again, without regard for what platform you'd be running on.
2. Now, imagine how your opponent would try to smear you. Without knowing every questionable thing you've done

in your life, how would they try to negatively portray your appearance and personality in front of voters?

3. How would you respond to those attacks? Do any of them have any merit? Are there things you should try to change about yourself to achieve your desired presence?

On Diversity

Companies benefit tremendously from the heterogeneity of their workforce. If everyone had the same background, as was once the case in many industries, thinking would become siloed and stagnant, and companies would be able to appeal only to audiences that matched their own internal culture. Studies show that diversity allows companies to be more progressive, nimble, creative, thoughtful, and productive.

Despite the progress being made, prejudice and stigma still exist. For many who don't fit the profile, getting in the door is hard, and that's just the first step. Of course, some workplaces are more welcoming and progressive than others, and if you count yourself as a minority in your ethnicity, gender, culture, beliefs, or presentation, I hope that you have found a workplace where you can be comfortable and safe, be accepted, and thrive. But odds are, at some point in our career, most of us are going to get judged against regressive standards by somebody in the workplace.

Sometimes, diversity refers to culture, ethnicity, gender, sexual orientation, or another more concrete difference, in which case there is no reason for anyone to change—acceptance is the only right or necessary response. Other times, diversity comes from a chosen style or look, and that person may choose to express themself in different ways depending on the situation. For instance, my doctor's medical assistant has both arms fully tattooed, but he wears long-sleeve shirts, or arm coverings if wearing short sleeves. I asked him, "Does the office require you

continued

to cover your arms?" He said, "No, I just prefer to do it so as not to make patients uncomfortable." I found that to be a self-aware, emotionally intelligent, empathetic perspective. He did not say it begrudgingly but comfortably and confidently.

On the other hand, if my doctor's medical assistant wore a hijab, it would be absolutely unacceptable for me or my doctor to ask them to remove it to make others comfortable. This is where comportment and acceptance can both be used as an opportunity to build bridges. If the medical assistant wearing a hijab approached patients with a warm, engaging attitude and made them feel at ease, anyone who came in with reservations would quickly feel differently. Likewise, by demonstrating appreciation for the medical assistant's care without regard to their culture, a comfortable and positive interaction can take place—there simply is no issue.

From a manager's point of view, if you are doing something they believe hurts morale, disrupts people, or repels customers or vendors, they have a right to discuss their policies and procedures with you. Most companies have a dress code, and you'll be made aware of it before you join. If you are, and you accept it at that time, you cannot expect to change and go against the policies once on board.

However, you do have a right to bring up suggestions for change as society changes. If you are put in the uncomfortable position of having to explain to your boss how they can be more inclusive, plan your presentation carefully. Remember that you are suggesting this change not only for yourself but for others who may have a similar problem, which can add strength to your case. Regardless of the answer your boss gives, thank them for their time, even if the result is not what you hoped for.

Racism still exists; this much is clear, and you may very well encounter it in your career. But when you do, it will likely be paired with an implicit threat of retaliation. It's critical to be respectful and tread lightly. If you need to keep your job, then your job is to keep your job, not to educate your boss. If the situation is bad enough that it affects your happiness, it's time to move on—quickly.

Virtual Brand

If this chapter has made you feel a bit self-conscious about being judged in person, dig in deep, because it's time to explore all the reasons you should feel the same way about your online presence. People will google you both before and after they meet you. Prospective employers may search your Facebook page as readily as your LinkedIn page. But, even if it seems like a catch-22, having no or little presence online won't help your executive presence, either. Executive presence includes an internet presence—one you can be proud of. Your virtual brand should send a message that is in line with your self-perception and the image you convey.

Your brand is really your reputation—your personal and career personas. If someone is going to interview you for a job, buy your services, allow you to date their daughter, or check you out for themselves, the first place they'll go for information is social media.

To solidify your online brand:

- Consider who is looking at it. If you are job hunting, recruiters and employers will look. If you got the job, peers are undoubtedly checking out the newest member of their team. If you have a side business in addition to your career, weigh whether you're comfortable with people from your professional life knowing this information.
- Be self-aware. Think about how people benefit from knowing you, and highlight those things. Think about your personal brand, your elevator pitch.
- Choose the social media platforms that fit your interests, your audience, and your experiences or background. You can create content across various platforms with adjustments that fit the platform.

- Use profile pictures that fit the media. Please don't damage your budding executive presence by using that picture from the cocktail party where a martini is obstructing your face and the person next to you is only half cropped from the shot. Invest in a head shot taken by a professional.
- Update your profile frequently. Stay current. As you gain information, skills, and credentials, and as you change jobs, make sure your profiles reflect those updates.
- Stay current with the larger conversation that's happening in your industry, and contribute to it. If you have a thoughtful opinion about something that people were tweeting about last week, people still want to hear it this week.
- Connect with those you have networked with.

Avoid posting personal opinions or controversial content—this is especially true on professional websites. When you post something, ask yourself first if it is:

- Relevant
- Engaging
- Positive
- Accurate
- Valuable
- Unique

Ask yourself what the function of your post is. Think about your intention. Do you want to:

- Stimulate conversations?
- Give insider information?
- Provide little-known information?
- Teach something or educate people?
- Channel traffic to specific content?

Every day we hear about another hack—assume nothing is safe:

- Check your privacy settings (but don't trust them).
- Change passwords frequently and use a password manager.
- Avoid using obvious information such as your name, birthday, or year of birth as a password.
- Don't reuse passwords.
- Be careful what you browse on a public or unsecured Wi-Fi network.
- Be aware that apps you use often have access to your social media information.

Digital hygiene, also called cyber or internet hygiene, is the practice of cleaning up and maintaining your digital world. This includes organizing your computer (e.g., filing like documents in folders and deleting outdated files and emails), setting strong passwords, using multifactor authentication, installing reputable antivirus and malware software, and keeping your hard drive clean. But it's also removing old posts or photos that don't represent the image you want to convey.

Virtual Brand Exercise: Digital Hygiene

- Organize your inbox and unsubscribe from junk emails.
- Update your devices, and delete old apps and accounts.
- Move everything into a password manager.
- Review privacy and security settings on accounts and social media.

Make it a practice to do this update once every quarter.

Virtual Brand Exercise: Social Media

- Make a list of people in your industry whom you follow online.
- Split them into two lists: people you don't like and people you respect.
- Unfollow everyone on the "don't like" list.
- Look at the bios of everyone on your "respect" list. What do they have in common? What digital conventions do they use? That is, what kinds of things do they post, and how do they communicate? Can you tell who they are from their bios, or are they obfuscating their identity?
- Update your profile or bio based on the best of what you've seen.

Virtual Brand Exercise: Google Yourself

- Put your name into Google or another search engine.
- Make a list of the top links that come up.
- How many of those links are about you, and how many are about someone else with the same name?
- How many of those links are items you put online yourself, and how many of them are things that are *about* you but not *by* you?

- How many of those links are directly relevant to your current career? What do these messages say about your competence in your current career?
- How many of those links are about other things in your life? Do they paint a well-rounded and interesting portrait of who you are?
- If there are any things that are negative or inaccurate, find the email of the person responsible for that website, and write them a polite invitation to have a conversation with you about it and about whether it should still be online or not. (Recognize that you might not prevail in that conversation, but often, people will remove the offending content rather than start a conflict.)

Reputation

While image is a combination of your self-image and the visual representation you make to others, your reputation is the general belief or opinion that other people hold about you. Your reputation is the way you are viewed by people: what they think of you, what you are known for, and how they label you—good, bad, or other.

A good reputation is a big determiner of your social standing and the measure of your influence in society. A good reputation is definitely associated with getting better jobs, taking on leadership roles, and being trusted. But a bad one—rather, a notorious one—can sometimes be better than none. For example, if you're known for having exacting, unreasonably high standards, you may be considered to possess a standard of excellence that equates to a great product or service. What you don't want, though, is people actively complaining about you behind your back.

Trust in reputation is very important to senior executives. They often tell me they prefer someone they can trust over someone with more competence whom they might not trust. Trust in this case means having integrity, honesty, and morality as well as being principled, ethical, and generally upright.

A good reputation comes from:

- Showing interest in and sincere empathy for others.
- Making work life more pleasant for others.
- Following words with actions.
- Demonstrating courage.
- Being decisive.
- Being honest and genuine.
- Being even-tempered.
- Being fun and interesting to be around.
- Setting a good example.
- Making amends and reparations; making the situation right.
- Slowing down and thinking ahead.
- Having an inexhaustible good nature.
- Showing thought, intelligence, and common sense.

A bad reputation comes from:

- Thinking you already know everything.
- Being intellectually lazy.
- Assigning blame.
- Thinking you are smarter than others.
- Not listening and learning.
- Being unwilling to admit you don't know something or ask questions.
- Abusing your power in any way.
- Acting superior to others.
- Divulging confidentialities.

- Bragging, boasting, and claiming credit.
- Thinking about yourself most of the time; failing to cultivate empathy.

You can ask people about your own reputation. One man had an eye-opening experience talking with his colleagues about his reputation. He said, "They didn't hold back. They were harsh, but it was what I needed to hear. If I recall exactly, they said things like, 'You lack humility, overestimate your capabilities, do not engage to learn so no one tells you things, and seem driven by ego, not purpose.' Well, it gave me a clear view of what to start working on. I have and I will continue until my last breath."

As you work to build and maintain your reputation, there will be things you can't control. Care about what you have control over—yourself and your own actions—and not about what others think, which isn't necessarily in your control. There will always be people who attack, criticize, and make fun of you because they are jealous or they are bullies. There may also be misunderstandings and misinterpretations of your behavior. All you can do is deliberately, persistently, and consistently do your best. After that, what people think is up to them, and there can be no regrets, because you gave it your best.

If you slip up and do something that causes your reputation to suffer, you're going to have to double and triple your efforts. Some people might hold it against you forever, but most people believe in forgiveness. Take responsibility for your actions, and apologize authentically and directly to everyone who was harmed. Then, put it behind you, focus on the future so it won't happen again, and step up your game.

You can make your apologies more powerful if you avoid routinely apologizing for things that weren't a big deal or weren't really your fault. If you go through life saying "sorry" as frequently as you say "thank you" or "excuse me" or "please," it's going to be harder for people to tell whether you are truly self-aware and contrite for bigger mistakes.

You will make mistakes—everyone does. That's part of being human. Your reputation isn't built around being flawless; it's formed around how you handle yourself, even with mistakes.

Reputation Exercise: Self-Assessment

Check off any of the following statements that apply to you:

- ☐ I am not sought out or taken seriously by colleagues and managers.
- ☐ I have the increasing sense that my intelligence and abilities aren't helping me advance in my career.
- ☐ I sense disregard for my authority by those above, below, or around me.
- ☐ I don't seem to be taking on new responsibilities at work, and it seems like my current responsibilities are being chipped away and micromanaged.
- ☐ My ideas aren't welcome.
- ☐ I experience indignities, such as being ignored in meetings, being left out of the loop on key decisions, and being omitted from important emails, meetings, and social gatherings.

We'll explore what you can do if you relate to any of these sentiments. But first, take a moment for self-compassion. Take a deep breath, sit up straight, and say to yourself, "I am valuable, competent, and intelligent. I have the ability to overcome any obstacle. And I am learning how."

Reputation Exercise: Reputation Perspectives

Answer these two questions:

- What would you want people to say to your parents about you?
- What would you like to read in the *Wall Street Journal* about yourself?

Then, ask trusted colleagues:

- What would you tell my parents about working with me?
- What do you think the *Wall Street Journal* would write about me?

Take responses with a grain of salt, as people may respond kindlier to you because they know you or don't want to offend you. But also, be compassionate toward yourself; if you let this exercise undermine your confidence, that could exacerbate the problems. You are capable of being your best self, and we are all works in progress. This test is merely designed to see how closely your self-image aligns with your reputation.

Reputation Exercise: Reputation Repair

- First, write down a sentence that describes the reputation that you want to have. Begin your statement with "I am" rather than "I want to be." It might read something like,

"I am reliable, hardworking, and accountable, but I'm also fun to be around and an empathetic colleague."

- Next, do a reality check. Think of one person at work—ideally, someone with whom you've had friction in the past, but whom you respect nonetheless—and write down a speculative sentence about what you fear they think about you. It might sound like, "She is a perfectionist who works too much and doesn't understand that the rest of us have lives outside work."
- Now go to that person, explain that you are working on yourself, and ask them what your reputation is. Ask them if they can come up with any specific instances from which aspects of your reputation stemmed.
- Write down a list of concrete actions you can take to rectify any negative perceptions.
- Repeat as necessary.

Style/Wardrobe

In a sense, clothes are the most superficial of all aspects of image and reputation. Anyone can put on a good suit of clothes and look like a stereotypical leader from a business magazine. But it's also one of the easiest things to change, if necessary. This is one area in which you don't really want or need to stand out in the colorful sense of the term; instead, you'll want to pay attention to what those you admire are wearing and dress to that level.

It's easy to acquire the look that fits your company culture, industry, and geographic climate. Watch what leaders in the company wear. Don't copy them, but use their style as a template. There's a saying: Don't dress for the job you have; dress for the job you want. This is one area where you don't want to stand out. It's a shallow reason to dismiss someone because of their clothes, but it happens.

Think of it this way: In every sport, there are uniforms. In many jobs and businesses, there are also uniforms, whether it's explicit or implicit. Executive presence involves dressing like part of the team. It's okay to add a personal touch of flair so you can feel good about yourself, but discretion is key.

People see your posture, face, grooming, and clothes roughly in that order, but they go through those judgments in a nanosecond. The way you look makes people draw conclusions, and they either want to know more about you or lose interest in you.

When job interviewing, you likely put in extra effort with your appearance. If you get hired from that interview, be assured that they are going to expect you to show up every day looking like you did in the interview, because that image is what they hired. That said, it's okay to overdress for an interview when in doubt. Better to show up in a suit even if you discover the office is generally business casual. After they hire you, they'll joke that you can lose the tie.

One of the best reasons to pay attention to your wardrobe is that what you wear deeply affects you, much more deeply than it affects those around you. You want to wear clothes that make you feel confident. That's why dress matters, even if you're working remotely. If you're not wearing pants during a video meeting, you're going to feel and act like you're not wearing pants. My advice here: Wear the pants.

Designers and brands understand that clothes and style affect your behavior. This quote from *Departures* magazine in an article about expensive watches is both humorous and telling: "A man, for example, wearing a mechanical watch that displays a lot of complications is communicating that he is possessed of an agile mind and part of an intellectual elite equipped to understand the mysteries of time."

Another statement touting the power of fashion appeared in *Vegas* magazine, which featured a designer's line of leather jackets: "I like to think of the man feeling like a warrior—of work, of love, of life—when he's wearing one of these pieces." In the interest of executive presence, you might take this as a disclaimer to wear the clothes; don't let them wear you.

The overarching point here is, dress smartly, but don't let your clothes be more interesting than you are. If your clothing is distracting in any way, it's going to be harder to get people to focus on what you're saying. All your clothes should say about you is that you are dressed for success.

Style/Wardrobe Exercise: Decipher Your Closet

This exercise will require some real objectivity on your part.

1. Go to your closet and pull out your work clothes.
2. Evaluate each piece as to what you might think of someone else if you saw them wearing it.
3. Think about your own motivation in purchasing that item. Did you see a person featured in *Forbes* wearing something similar, or was it a Kardashian? Was it on sale and that was the motivation?

The point is to think about why you have a piece and what message it sends. Most people in the public eye have someone who puts together their look, enabling them to appear exactly as they wish to be viewed. You and I don't have that luxury, but we can use an objective eye to put together our own look.

Style/Wardrobe Exercise: Go Out, Two Ways

Pick a restaurant or store. One day, dress in your best business clothes, and visit that restaurant or store. Carry yourself with good posture and comportment.

Another day, go to the same place wearing your grungiest clothes, but maintain that good posture and comportment.

Pay attention to how you are treated each time. Pay attention to how you feel in your skin. You may or may not be treated the same, but you will likely feel differently each time.

Style/Wardrobe Exercise: Executive Review

1. Choose your favorite three work ensembles, from shirt to shoes. Include all your favorite accessories.
2. One outfit at a time, try them on. Stand before a full-length mirror.
3. Pretend you are the top executive at your company looking at you. Look with a critical eye toward the clothing. Does it fit properly? Is it worn or faded or pilling? Are your shoes scuffed or stretched out?
4. If your assessment is unfavorable, dig deeper in your closet to find a new ensemble that works better.
5. Make a promise to mix up your outfits and wear something new and fresh at least once a week. Replace any ill-fitting or worn pieces.

Takeaways

- The appearance you try to project in your image should be as close to who you truly are as possible. Executive presence is not about trying to appear as someone you aren't; rather, it's about being confident in your appearance.
- Your reputation is the best business asset you can own.
- Your reputation exists whether you do anything about it or not. But there is much you can do to protect and maintain it. Ultimately, endeavor to actually be what you want to appear to be.
- Refrain from judging others by their looks, habits, and appearances. Let them show their true colors in their words and deeds.
- Look at your digital brand as a reflection of you. Choose your posts and pictures wisely. Update your profile frequently.
- Dress for the job you want, not for the job you have. Your clothes should say "dressed for success."

CHAPTER SEVEN

Authenticity

The path to success looks different for everyone, and you must follow yours, even if you use similar executive presence tools as those who've achieved success before you.

You are starting with your unique brand. You're a good person: responsible, honest, and fair. You know yourself; lean into that. Lean into your particular leadership style, into constantly improving your communication and building relationships. Work to align your physical comportment and appearance with the image you have of yourself and the reputation that you want to build and maintain. You're on your way.

In this final chapter, we'll look at finding your own executive presence, identify some roadblocks you might encounter, and explore how you can adjust your approach as situations change.

Finding Your Presence

It's good to watch others you admire and respect to observe what they do and how they do it. You want to pick the best of what you see and add some of these strategies to your own style for yourself. To be clear, you don't watch people with executive presence in order to copy them but rather to observe the effectiveness of their behavior. When you see the actions and outcomes you want to emulate, pick them up and see how they can be modified to work with your own personality.

All social interactions require a blend of conformity and individuality. Interestingly, the more conformity you adhere to in your presence, the more freedom you'll get. If you walk, talk, and dress like people expect a successful executive to, you can then do something quite different and get away with it.

That's how positive conformity gives you freedom. When you use expected social manners and dress in the uniform for your profession, you make people comfortable around you. That same positive conformity brings together people who come from different backgrounds; it's a bridge of similarity that unites you in working together.

When you strengthen social bonds in this way and gain acceptance, it opens you up for the chance to say and do what you think is best. When you know yourself, what you stand for, what you won't stand for, and what you want in life, you can use this to help grow your emotional intelligence.

Positive conformity isn't worrying about what people think about you and then trying to please them. Rather, it is about developing good habits by observing positive traits of others and abandoning bad habits that hold you back. It builds confidence and helps you face the unknown with a sense of opportunity. You have a guide, a system, a rule to fall back on when you adhere to the expected behavior.

Confidently knowing yourself and not trying to change or hide who you are increases your self-worth. With that, you:

- Are more fun to be around.
- Don't get jealous of others.
- Have more courage.
- Are more decisive.
- Don't fear mistakes.
- Aren't easily embarrassed.
- Accept the inevitability of moments of self-doubt (everyone has them).
- Won't lose self-control.
- Take necessary action, even when you are nervous.

More than one CEO has told me a version of this statement: "I've had many years of having to bluff my way through. I just danced around with confidence. Down deep, I was churning with anxiety." Others have told me something along the lines of this: "I do what every other CEO does: Go into a dark room, bend over, vomit, straighten myself up, and go back out there." The point is this: We are all still human, even at the top.

Conversely to positive conformity, negative conformity is anything that:

- Causes you to lose your identity.
- Hampers your personal progress.
- Makes you dependent on others' thinking.
- Makes you apathetic.
- Deprives you of diversity in your thinking and relationships.
- Causes harm to others.

Being forced to participate in a toxic workplace or be party to unethical behaviors are obvious examples of negative conformity. However, negative conformity can also stem from situations such as an atmosphere of prejudice or inequality, poor or lacking leadership, or unfavorable working conditions.

Finding Your Presence Exercise: Role Models

At the beginning of this book, we explored the profiles of three leaders: Chris Lighty, Mary Barra, and Dr. Renee Dua. If you had the opportunity to write this book, who would you choose to profile? Write your own list of three people, making sure to focus on different types of individuals in contrasting industries.

Write at least one of those profiles. In about 800 words, how would you explain who that person is, what they have achieved, and how their executive presence shines through/is most notable? What lessons would you take from them?

Don't keep that piece of writing to yourself! Write and rewrite; make it good enough that you want to share it with your friends or family or even online.

Finding Your Presence: Flip Your Routine

Ditch your routine during an ordinary day. Some examples:
- If you've been sitting when talking to someone on the phone, stand.
- If you've been teaching or training someone, go learn something for yourself.
- If you've been talking a lot, be quiet and listen.
- If you've been listening, speak up.

- If you have bad news to dispense, instead of procrastinating, bring it up, along with some solutions if possible, before the recipient hears it from someone else.
- If you've been serious lately, bring in a little humor.

Seek out the opposite in everything you can. Your goal is to stretch yourself while still remaining within the scope of acceptable behavioral norms.

Roadblocks

By making the choice to develop your executive presence, you will engage in lots of rewarding interactions and get positive reinforcement from those around you. You may wonder why you hadn't tried for this kind of personal development before. But just as when you learn anything new, you will likely encounter some roadblocks. Here are some possibilities.

Some People Will Be Jealous of Your Efforts.

One, because they aren't making changes themselves, and two, because you are. How can you tell if somebody is envious of you? They might act friendly but fight against you behind your back, downplay some achievement you've made, or talk disparagingly about you, even telling lies.

When this happens, keep your emotions in check. Reflect on your own self-awareness and use your self-control. Tell yourself, "It's human nature for envy to occur. I need to remember my goals and why I'm trying to change and develop. I'll do what I need to do with dignity and civility, without causing damage to the self-esteem of others who are trying to do that to me."

As long as their behavior does not negatively impact your work, try to ignore it. If it's egregious, address it. You might privately say to the person, "Did I do something to upset you? I get the feeling that you are not a big fan of mine. Do you want to tell me why?" This kind of statement requires them to explain their poor behavior. They will likely be caught off guard and may respond by backpedaling and denying any hard feelings. This gentle approach also puts them on warning that you are aware of their behavior and that their passive-aggressive approach is not a secret. They may also open up. If they do, listen without interrupting. If you learn something helpful that will make you better, take it and say, "Thanks for telling me." If the issue is petty, inaccurate, or harmful, explain, "You can behave however you want. You are an individual doing what you need to do. There is one thing I will not tolerate, however, and that is allowing anyone else to cause me to fail to perform well. You are doing that now. I am happy to try to clear this up with you. If you don't think we can, we can take it to the manager to get their take on things."

The important thing is to say all of this in an even tone and with a relaxed facial expression. Don't show any sign of animosity, anger, or lack of emotional control. In the end, the problem may never completely go away, but you can at least feel good that you addressed it.

You Will Wonder If You're Doing Things Right Because You Don't Get Enough Feedback.

Many managers tell me, "I can't hold people's hands. I can't coddle them and make them feel good. If they do something wrong, I'll tell them, but if they do something right, I assume that is what they are paid to do." Perhaps not the most productive or empowering management philosophy, this common statement illustrates the big-picture viewpoint many managers have—maybe due to overwork, maybe due to a lack of empathy or people skills, but indicative of the need for workers to read between the lines.

What that means is, you'll know in your heart if you are making progress in your executive presence efforts. How? You're noticed more by centers of influence. You're included in meetings and cc'd on emails, asked your opinion, or maybe given a stretch assignment.

You may not get applause or kudos for an achievement. Sometimes it's because people didn't notice, weren't aware of the difficulty, don't know all the work that was put in, or simply have a lot of other things on their plate and are too busy to say "thank you." You may have a manager like that, but you don't want to be a manager like that.

To recognize others, and to get them recognized by the entire organization, tell a brief story around the achievement in a follow-up email or by speaking up in a meeting. Give credit for the success to others and simply get it on the record so people are aware. You can self-promote with self-respect. By complimenting the efforts of others, you shine a light on your own achievements.

You Will Make Mistakes.

No matter how hard you try, no matter your best intent, you will mess up. Immediately, or as soon as possible, own up to it. Do not hide, dismiss, or lay blame elsewhere. Apologize to anyone affected in a face-to-face conversation or one-to-one on the phone. Follow any apologetic email or text with a conversation. Fix the mistake as soon as you can and as well as you can, and ask for help from those who can assist in this repair. Check with all parties involved to make sure you have remedied the error. If not, do something about that.

If there is general agreement that you took care of the problem, reflect on what led to you making that mistake, where your information was from, what data you lacked, what you should have done but didn't do, and what you will do differently next time. Share these takeaways with people involved and invite them to either add their feedback or confirm that you are on target.

When all is done, don't make that mistake again. You can make a different one—that's part of life—but don't repeat ones you've made. And go on fearlessly.

Roadblocks Exercise: Resolve Your Own Jealousy

The purpose of this exercise is to address your own jealous feelings and try to remove them. Then focus on the object of your jealousy and consider how you can make them look good and maintain their self-esteem, to counter jealousy they may get from others.

- Think about someone in your life right now whom you might have reason to be jealous of.
- Consider where those feelings come from and why. Write them down. They become clearer in written form. Then burn the paper.
- Go to the person and sincerely praise them on their accomplishment. Ask them to tell you about it—how they did it and what, if anything, they would do differently next time.
- Tell someone else about that person's accomplishment. Brag them up.

Roadblocks Exercise: Practice Mistakes

Don't wait for a mistake to happen to follow those steps.

Look at situations in your company that were missteps and walk yourself through the same process as if it were a mistake you were involved in:

- Identify the mistake.
- Think about how you would accept ownership.
- Choose the words you would use to apologize.
- Study what caused it: when, how, what, why.
- Walk through fixing the problem in your mind.
- Check, in an empathetic fashion, to see if it did get fixed in others' minds.

The idea is to think through situations you might encounter before they occur. Because you have no emotional involvement, you can think more clearly and set a precedent for managing your emotions in an instance when you are involved.

I remember meeting the chief of staff of a CEO. I asked him how he handles mistakes with his boss. He said, "My job is to catch my mistakes before I make them."

Adjusting

Effective executives are not developed overnight. The task you've undertaken is not easy, nor is it necessarily a speedy trip. If it were, more people would do it. Many don't because they won't put the effort in. But you will.

Right there you set yourself apart from others. That's your start, and it's a good one: You're thinking and doing something about your desire to be more memorable, impressive, credible, genuine, trusted, cool, calm, collected, comfortable, confident, and competent. You want to get useful things done with considerable civility through the combined efforts of people while always trying to maintain the self-esteem of those around you.

Every day, think about proactive steps you can take toward building your executive presence.

- Think about some business, political, or community leader you admire and study the person's presence: how they treat others, how they talk about themselves, and how they dress, walk, and talk. Ask yourself what causes you to admire that individual, then make a pledge to yourself to try out for yourself what they are doing. Do this with the awareness that you will modify admirable qualities to fit yourself as you go.

- Think about that person's leadership style and how it works with the organization at the time. Think about how it might need to change: why, when, and how. Consider the leadership style you are leaning toward, and weigh its pros and cons as it relates to your organization's needs and your own personality.

- Think about your own motivations, your strengths and weaknesses, and what you need to do to improve. Take one area and plot out what you can do on a daily basis to improve. The goal is not to be overly critical. Practice deep acceptance of what you bring to the table. Remind yourself that you are more than adequate to handle what comes your way. Always choose a productive, constructive perspective of how you will make a change today.

- Think about others. Ask yourself, what's in this for them? What do they want to achieve, maintain, or avoid? What would they want from me? How can I give them what they need while maintaining my own objectives?

- Think how you can improve in every aspect of your communication, both in person and virtually, as well as verbally and in writing. Communication is all we have. We do it whether we think about it or not. Words, tone, pace, body language—they all help you build relationships, or they cause conflict. It's up to your choice of words and actions.
- Think about your clothes and appearance and how they support your personal brand—or not.
- Work on building and maintaining your reputation, which is your doing. If you don't like what it's been in the past, every day is a new day to change the trajectory of how others will view you.

The only way to have a really good, long-lasting reputation with executive presence is to, on one hand, work on the unwritten code as laid out in this book and, on the other hand, know and retain your true self. Be willing to develop your true self through new information, too. Then clasp those hands together. That will give you sustained success in your endeavors.

We are all works in progress, adjusting and growing for a lifetime. The adjustment required for executive presence involves altering your mindset and your behavior, perhaps only slightly, in order to achieve the desired behavior, appearance, or result. You can be true to yourself while you change.

The circumstances of the world are so variable that even if you didn't want to change, change is needed all the time just to remain the same. This isn't easy, but it beats the alternative, because if you don't embrace new opportunities and behaviors, you will fall behind, or new problems will compound as you progress in your career. It's not just where you are but in what direction you are moving.

Adjustment Exercise: Reflection

1. Think about and make note of changes you have already made in your thoughts and actions since starting this book. Rank, on a scale of 1 to 5 (5 is highest), how effective you've become in self-awareness, self-control, empathy, communication, image, and any other area.
2. List the areas you still want to work on. In a month, re-rank your success.
3. In six months, look at both lists and re-rank the areas. At this point, your goal should be to rank behaviors at a 4 or 5.
4. Take note and pat yourself on the back for any advancement you've achieved. And, in areas where you are still at a 1 or 2, put extra effort in for another month, then re-rank.
5. By checking and rechecking, you'll be able to keep track of what you are working on, and you'll have the opportunity to notice and take pride in how much you've accomplished.

Adjustment Exercise: Collect Feedback

1. Ask three confidants what they think you're best at.
2. Ask them if they have seen any changes in your behavior.
3. Ask them what changes they think you should be making.

Basically, you're looking to see if they have taken notice of the changes you've made in your efforts to build executive presence, but you're also going to get their opinions on your strengths and weaknesses. Take their responses with a grain of salt, because they see you through their own lenses of strengths and weaknesses. But in all of this, look for nuggets of truth, too.

Takeaways

- If you act like people expect a successful executive to act, you can then do something different and get away with it—this is where conformity and individuality converge.
- When you know yourself, what you stand for and won't, and what you want, you can use this to grow your emotional intelligence—and authenticity.
- Look to those you admire to observe behaviors you'd like to emulate. In turn, the greatest use of your authenticity is to inspire others to behave in a similar way. You are being watched by managers above, peers alongside, and rising stars below all the time. Accustom people to the real and always improving version of yourself.
- Face your mistakes head-on, learn from them, but don't make the same mistakes again.
- Continue to learn from others, even about yourself, as seen through their eyes.

Conclusion

We've talked about a lot, but if there is one all-important message to leave you with, it is the reminder to use all these tools consistently and never stop, even when you reach the top. Some skills may come more naturally, and others may take work, but all these tools are needed for true executive presence. Intelligence, hard work, and honesty are good, but they are not enough.

Make yourself a lifelong learner—there is always more to be understood and gained. You will be ahead of your competition if every day you catch yourself thinking at least one time, *How can I add to my executive presence today to be a better leader?* If you do that every day for a year, including weekends, you'll have 365 habit-changing experiences.

This is your choice and your chance to shine. You have the tools—use them all, consistently, and you will enjoy a rewarding career with you as the driver of your destiny.

Resources

Doug Conant, president, ConantLeadership.com. Former CEO of Campbell's Soup, recognized as a leadership consultant who has actually been a CEO.

Tom O'Malley, president, Grow Well Company. Strategy and leadership development.

D. A. Benton, president, Benton Management Resources, Inc. Ranked as one of the top 10 executive coaches in the country.

Nancy Wilhelms, strategist, Nancy Wilhelms Consulting, author of *Yes! You Can Do It! The Young Woman's Guide to Starting a Fulfilling Career*, Smoke Tree Press, 2021.

Pete Wehry, president, Full Court Leadership. Leadership coaching for sports pros.

Bob Berkowitz, president, Bob Berkowitz Communications Consultants. Former White House correspondent for NBC.

Dean Campos, founder, Clear Legend. Millennial mentorship.

Ann Clarke, president, Colorado Women of Influence, Inc. Leading organization for women executives.

Jack Falvey, president, MakingtheNumbers.com. Lifelong marketing guru, leadership author, and *Wall Street Journal* contributor.

Virginia Johnson, founder, Charisma Crash Course. Commonsense lessons for every walk of life.

Cynthia Leibrock, president, AgingBeautifully.org. Living a healthy, fulfilled life for your entire life.

References

Chapter 1

Brilliant, Ashleigh. *I May Not Be Totally Perfect, but Parts of Me Are Excellent*. Santa Barbara, CA: Woodbridge Press Publishing Company, 1979.

Colby, Laura. *Road to Power: How GM's Mary Barra Shattered the Glass Ceiling*. Hoboken, NJ: John Wiley & Sons, Inc., 2015.

Colvin, Geoff. "Mary Barra's (Unexpected) Opportunity." *Fortune*, September 18, 2014. Fortune.com/2014/09/18/mary-barra-general-motors.

Feloni, Richard. "GM CEO Mary Barra Said the Recall Crisis of 2014 Forever Changed Her Leadership Style." *Business Insider*, November 14, 2018. BusinessInsider.com/gm-mary-barra-recall-crisis-leadership-style-2018-11.

Foroohar, Rana. "Mary Barra's Bumpy Ride at the Wheel of GM." *Time*, September 25, 2014. Time.com/magazine/us/3429641/october-6th-2014-vol-184-no-13-u-s.

Hoffman, Reid. "Rapid Response: GM's Mary Barra: 'Going Ventilator Fast.'" June 13, 2020. In *Masters of Scale with Reid Hoffman*, podcast.

Mogul. "The Life and Times of Reggie Ossé." August 29. 2019. In *Mogul*, podcast. GimletMedia.com/shows/mogul/76h97x/the-life-and-times-of-reggie-oss.

Muller, Joann. "Exclusive: Inside New CEO Mary Barra's Urgent Mission to Fix GM." *Forbes*, May 28, 2014. Forbes.com/sites/joannmuller/2014/05/28/exclusive-inside-mary-barras-urgent-mission-to-fix-gm/?sh=76dab4d71c3a.

Smith, Danyel. "Remembering Chris Lighty, Hip-Hop Leader and My Friend." Last modified August 31, 2012. NPR.org/scctions/therecord/2012/08/31/160357103/remembering-chris-lighty-hip-hop-leader-and-my-friend.

Wall Street Journal. "Chris Lighty and Blue Williams—the Dynamic Duo of Urban Music." Last modified September 13, 2012. YouTube.com /watch?v=-HF7eyMXW3A.

Chapter 2

Brilliant, Ashleigh. *Appreciate Me Now and Avoid the Rush.* Santa Barbara, CA: Woodbridge Press Publishing Company, 1981.

Brilliant, Ashleigh. *I Have Abandoned My Search for Truth, and Am Now Looking for a Good Fantasy.* Santa Barbara, CA: Woodbridge Press Publishing Company, 1980.

Bullwinkle, Kristeen. "Commanding Leaders: DISC D style Leadership." Last modified October 3, 2018. DiSCProfiles.com/blog/2018/10 /commanding-leadership/#.YCrVsmhKg2w.

Eure Consulting. "Leadership Styles: Commanding." Last modified June 7, 2019. EureConsulting.com/leadership-styles-commanding.

Indeed.com. "14 Traits of Visionary Leaders." Indeed Career Guide. Last modified December 3, 2020. Indeed.com/career-advice /career-development/traits-of-visionary-leadership.

Janse, B. "Coaching Leadership Style." Toolshero. Last modified 2018. Toolshero.com/leadership/coaching-leadership-style.

Leadership Ahoy! "Pacesetting Leadership—What Is It? Pros/Cons? Examples?" LeadershipAhoy.com/pacesetting-leadership-what-is -it-pros-cons-examples.

Ramamoorthy, Ajay. "Why Pacesetting Leadership is Not Always Toxic." July 2019. Upshotly.com.

STU Online. "What Is Democratic/Participative Leadership? How Collaboration Can Boost Morale." Last modified June 1, 2018. online .STU.edu/articles/education/democratic-participative-leadership .aspx.

Wilson, Graham. "5 Ways Affiliative Leadership Boosts Team Performance." TheSuccessFactory.co.uk/blog/reasons-affiliative -leadership-boosts-team-performance.

Chapter 3

Blue, Alexis. "Poor Social Skills May be Harmful to Mental and Physical Health." The University of Arizona. Last modified November 6, 2017. news.Arizona.edu/story/poor-social-skills-may-be-harmful -mental-and-physical-health.

Kennedy-Moore, Eileen. "What Are Social Skills?" *Psychology Today*, August 18, 2011. PsychologyToday.com/us/blog/growing-friendships /201108/what-are-social-skills.

Lawson, Loraine. "Emotional Intelligence: What You Don't Know May Cost Both You and Your Company." *TechRepublic*. Last modified May 11, 2000. TechRepublic.com/article/emotional -intelligence-what-you-dont-know-may-cost-both-you-and-your -company.

Peters, Ben. "Deep Breathing Is the Ultimate Self-Control." Creator Villa. Last modified November 30, 2019. CreatorVilla.com/2019 /11/30/deep-breathing-is-the-ultimate-self-control.

Webb, Jennifer. "10 Benefits of Self-Awareness and How it Can Impact Your Life." Contentment Questing. Accessed on April 21, 2020. ContentmentQuesting.com/benefits-of-self-awareness.

Chapter 4

Brain Labs Digital. "The Guide to Find Your Brand's Tone of Voice." BrainLabsDigital.com/marketing-library/the-guide-to-finding -your-brands-tone-of-voice.

Cranston, Allen. "7 Tips How to Manage and Resolve Conflict in the Workplace." HRCloud.com. Last modified February 3, 2020. HRCloud.com/blog/7-tips-on-how-to-manage-and-resolve-conflict -in-the-workplace.

McKay, Dawn Rosenberg. "6 Topics to Avoid Discussing at Work." Last modified November 20, 2019. TheBalanceCareers.com/topics -to-avoid-discussing-at-work-526267.

Neely, Pamella. "7 Storytelling Techniques and How to Apply Them." Last modified August 25, 2014. PracticalECommerce.com/7 -storytelling-techniques-and-how-to-apply-them.

O'Hara, Carolyn. "How to Tell a Great Story." *Harvard Business Review*, July 30, 2014. HBR.org/2014/07/how-to-tell-a-great-story.

Rochow, Michael. "9 Strategies for Building Better Professional Relationships." GetHppy.com/workplace-happiness/building -professional-relationships.

Spacey, John. "9 Examples of Nonverbal Communication." Last modified September, 5, 2017. Simplicable.com/new/nonverbal-communication.

Chapter 5

Ash, Eve. "What Is Business Etiquette?" *SmartCompany*, July 11, 2019. SmartCompany.com.au/people-human-resources/business-etiquette.

Cohen, Arianne. *The Tall Book: A Celebration of Life on High*. New York: Bloomsbury, 2009.

D'Angelo, Matt. "International Business Etiquette from Around the World." Last modified February 25, 2020. Business.com /articles/so-international-business-etiquette-from-around-the -world.

Lesbian, Gay, Bisexual, Transgender, Queer Plus (LGBTQ+) Resource Center. "Gender Pronouns." UWM.edu/lgbtrc/support/gender -pronouns.

Chapter 6

Brookins, Laurie. "A Son Shines." *Vegas*, 2019.

Departures.com. "Wrist Watch/Style Etc." 2019.

McKnight, David A. "What's Your Image Saying About You?" Last modified October 10, 2016. Medium.com/personal-growth/whats -your-image-saying-about-you-30293ba7cd98.

Chapter 7

Jilani, Zaid. "How Conformity Can Be Good and Bad for Society." Last modified May 30, 2019. GreaterGood.Berkeley.edu/article /item/how_conformity_can_be_good_and_bad_for_society.

Regoli, Natalie. "15 Biggest Pros and Cons of Conformity in Society." Last modified January 3, 2019. ConnectUSFund.org/15-biggest -pros-and-cons-of-conformity-in-society.

Index

M

Manners, 92–93, 95. *See also* Business etiquette
Mistakes, 135–136, 137
Motivation, 46–50
Musk, Elon, 14

N

Names, guidelines for, 91–92, 94–95
Networking challenge, 80
Nonverbal communication, 97–101
Nooyi, Indra, 22

O

Online presence, 113–117

P

Pace-setting leaders, 23–25
Page, Larry, 22
Parks, Rosa, 39
Personal brand, 108–110
Perspectives
    acknowledging different, 69–70
    reputation, 121
Posture, 102–104
Presence, 7, 130–133. *See also* Executive presence; Online presence

Q

Questions, asking
    about customs, 94
    about empathy, 55
    about motivation, 48–50
    about self-management/regulation, 43–44

R

Regulation, 39–44
Reinhold, Barbara Bailey, 33
Relationships, building and improving, 78–80
Reputation, 117–122
Roadblocks, encountering, 133–137
Role models, 132
Routines, flipping, 132–133

S

Schmidt, Eric, 22
Segrin, Chris, 56
Self-awareness, 34–35, 37–38
Self-management, 39–44
Smity, Danyel, 3
Social media, 116. *See also* Virtual brand
Social skills, 55–59. *See also* Business etiquette
Solso, Tim, 4
Storytelling, 65–70
Style/wardrobe, 122–125

T

Team-building analogy exercise, 68–69
Tone, of voice, 62–65
Toxic Work (Reinhold), 33
Trust, 118

V

Verbal communication,
70, 72–73, 75–76
Virtual brand, 113–117
Virtual workplaces, 96–97
Visionary leaders, 14–16

W

Welch, Jack, 24
West, Cornel, 107
Written communication,
71–72, 74–75

Z

Zuckerberg, Mark, 13, 14

About the Author

D. A. Benton has more than 30 years of international experience, partnering with, developing, and advancing the careers of executives in how they think, manage, and lead. She is ranked as one of the top 10 executive coaches in the world. She regularly presents keynote speeches to her client corporations that include Microsoft, American Express, Lockheed Martin, PepsiCo, and other leading global brands.

She is an award-winning *New York Times*-bestselling author on professional development and leadership with 12 books, including: *The Introvert's Guide to Networking, The Leadership Mind Switch, The CEO Difference, The Virtual Executive, How to Think Like a CEO, Secrets of a CEO, How to Act Like a CEO, Executive Charisma, CEO Material*, and *Lions Don't Need to Roar.*

In addition to books, Debra has written on leadership for *Harvard Business Review, Wall Street Journal, Bloomberg Businessweek*, and *Fast Company.*

CPSIA information can be obtained
at www.ICGtesting.com
Printed in the USA
JSHW060031011122
32375JS00010B/98